ALASKA SHRIMP & CRAB RECIPES

By Cecilia Nibeck

AK Enterprises
Anchorage, Alaska

ALASKA
SHRIMP and CRAB RECIPES
By Cecilia Nibeck

P.O. BOX 210241
ANCHORAGE, ALASKA 99521-0241

Acknowledgements

ILLUSTRATIONS
RED RAVEN DESIGN

PRODUCTION ASSISTANCE
CLASSIC DESIGN AND TYPOGRAPHY
KRYS HOLMES

PRINTED BY EVERBEST PRINTING CO., LTD., NANSHA, CHINA, THROUGH ALASKA PRINT BROKERS, ANCHORAGE, ALASKA.

ISBN # 0-9622117-4-5

109876

PREFACE

Nobody knows who the first person was to ever crack open a crab shell, or peel a shrimp, and taste the succulent meat inside. What would possess a person to pry apart the legs of a creature that looks like a marine insect, and eat what was found inside? Yet shrimp and crab are the world's favorite seafoods. In America, shrimp is second only to tuna in seafood consumption.

We collected these recipes from kitchens everywhere to bring you our idea of the versatility and delicacy of these wonderful seafoods. From the haughtiest restaurants of Paris to the campsite grill on Homer spit, shrimp and crab bring the succulent flavor of the exotic ocean to the world's taste buds.

They also are the tastiest way to sample foods of many different countries. Here you'll find recipes for Mediterranean, French Caribbean, Cajun, Italian, Tex-Mex, California-style, and traditional Alaskan dishes that you can make with just about any species of shrimp or crab is available to you.

As Cecilia and I prepared these recipes, they became a symbol of the variety, richness and piquancy of living. The tasty dishes that follow feature flavors, seasonings and preparation styles from many lands, but the meat of these dishes is pure wonder. This is the flesh of another world, a world beyond our and yet so full of blessings and gifts for us to enjoy throughout our lives.

This cookbook was one of Cecilia's last projects. She died in the summer of 1995, after twenty years in Alaska. Our life together was as succulent and well seasoned as any meal ever prepared. We took much pleasure compiling this book, and we hope it will bring grace and gusto into your lives as well.

Stu Nibeck
February 1, 1996

TABLE OF CONTENTS

Appetizers

Salads

Soup

Sandwiches

Main Dishes

CRAB

Salads

Soup

Sandwiches

Main Dishes

SHRIMP

PREPARING SHRIMP

Here are some quick tips on preparing shrimp for cooked shrimp. Shrimp may be boiled then shelled and deveined or shelled, and then boiled.

BOILED SHRIMP BEFORE SHELLING

1 1/2 pounds raw shrimp
1 quart water
1/4 cup salt

Wash shrimp. Place in boiling salted water. Simmer five minutes or until the shrimp float to the surface. Drain and rinse with cold water to stop cooking. Shell and remove sand veins. Rinse and chill.
Yields 3/4 pound cooked, shelled and deveined shrimp.

BOILED SHRIMP AFTER SHELLING

1 1/2 pounds shrimp
1 1/2 quart water
2 tablespoons salt

Shell shrimp. Make a shallow cut lengthwise down the back of each shrimp. Rinse and place in boiling salted water. Cover and return to boiling. Simmer for three to five minutes. Drain and rinse with cold water. Remove and sand vein particles. Chill.
Yields 3/4 pound cook shrimp.

BACON WRAPPED SHRIMP

16 large raw shrimp, shelled
8 thin strips of bacon, split lengthwise
2 eggs, lightly beaten
1/2 cup milk
1/2 cup flour seasoned with salt, pepper and garlic salt
oil for deep frying

Wrap each shrimp with bacon and secure with a toothpick. Beat eggs and milk. Dip shrimp into egg mixture then roll in seasoned flour. Deep fry shrimp until golden brown. Drain and serve hot.

Serves four.

CAJUN DIP

1 pound small cooked shrimp, shelled
1/4 cup butter
1 cup onion, chopped
2 cloves garlic, minced
1 can mushroom soup
8 ounces cheddar cheese, shredded
1 (4-ounce) can mushrooms, drained and chopped
2 packages (10 ounces each) frozen chopped broccoli
1 tablespoon hot pepper sauce
1 teaspoon salt
1 cup cashews, chopped
1 (6 ounce) can water chestnuts, sliced

Sauté onion and garlic in butter until tender. Add remaining ingredients. Cook over low heat for 15 minutes.
Serve hot.
Serves ten.

COLD MARINATED SHRIMP

2 pounds cooked shrimp, shelled
1/8 teaspoon red pepper, crushed
1 cup fresh lime juice
1 teaspoon salt
2 bay leaves
1/4 teaspoon cumin seeds
1 medium red onion, sliced and separated into rings
1/4 cup black olives, pitted and cut in halves.

Combine all ingredients, except shrimp, in a large bowl. Add shrimp. Cover and refrigerate overnight.
Serves ten.

CURRIED SHRIMP PUFFS

1/2 cup cooked shrimp, shelled and chopped
1 egg white
 pinch of salt
1/2 teaspoon curry powder

Beat egg white until stiff. Fold in other ingredients. Pile mixture on crackers. Put the crackers on a pan and broil until puffed and brown.
Serves two.

EASY MARINATE SHRIMP

**1 pound cooked shrimp, shelled and deveined
1 cup Miracle Whip
1 onion, sliced thin
juice of 1/2 lemon**

Pat shrimp dry to remove all moisture. Combine remaining ingredients. Pour over shrimp and refrigerate at least 24 hours.

Serves eight.

EASY SHRIMP DIP

**1 (4 1/2 ounce) can shrimp, drained and chopped
8 ounces cream cheese
16 ounce sour cream
1 package Italian dressing mix
2 tablespoon lemon juice**

Mix ingredients and chill several hours before serving.
Makes two cups.

FRESH SHRIMP PASTE

2 pounds cooked shrimp, shelled and chopped
1/2 cup wine vinegar
1/2 pound soft butter
1/2 teaspoon mace
1 teaspoon onion juice
fresh parsley, chopped
salt to taste

Cream shrimp with butter, mace and onion juice. Add salt to taste. Garnish with parsley.

Serve with crackers or toast.

HOT AND SPICY SHRIMP

3 pounds raw shrimp with shells
10 peppercorns
4 cloves garlic
1 teaspoon whole cloves
3 lemons, sliced
1/4 teaspoon cayenne pepper
1 large green pepper, chopped
4 bay leaves
1 tablespoon salt
1 teaspoon celery seed
1 cup vinegar
1 1/2 gallons water

Combine all ingredients, except the shrimp, in a large pot and bring to a boil. Boil for 15 minutes. Add shrimp and cover. Simmer for eight minutes. Drain and serve immediately.
Serves five.

HOT MARINATED SHRIMP

3 pounds raw shrimp, unshelled
3 quarts water
1 large onion, quartered
1/2 lemon, sliced
4 celery stalks
1/2 cup dry white wine
1 teaspoon basil leaves, crumbled
1/2 teaspoon thyme leaves, crumbled
2 bay leaves
4 cloves garlic, split
1 teaspoon basil leaves, crumbled
hot pepper to taste

Combine all ingredients, except for shrimp, in a large pot and bring to a boil. Add shrimp. Return to boiling and simmer for five minutes. Drain and serve hot.

Serves twelve.

HOT SHRIMP DIP

1 pound raw shrimp, shelled and chopped
1/2 cup butter
1/2 cup green onion, chopped
1/4 green pepper, chopped
1 pound mild cheddar cheese, diced
1 tablespoon dry sherry
1/2 cup bottled chili sauce
1 tablespoon Worcestershire sauce
1-2 drops hot pepper sauce
pepper to taste

Combine shrimp with butter, green pepper, and onion in medium sauce pan. Sauté shrimp for five minutes. In a different pan, combine cheese, sherry, chili sauce, pepper, hot pepper sauce and Worcestershire sauce. Heat slowly to melt cheese. Combine shrimp and cheese mixtures. Heat through.

Makes three cups.

PICKLED SHRIMP

2 1/2 pounds raw shrimp in shells
1/2 cup celery tops
1/4 cup mixed pickling spices
1 tablespoon salt
2 cups onions, sliced
7 bay leaves
1 1/2 cup oil
3/4 cup white vinegar
3 tablespoons capers and juice
2 1/2 teaspoons celery seed
1 1/2 teaspoons salt
hot pepper to tastes

Cover shrimp with boiling water. Add celery, pickling spices and salt. Cover and simmer for five minutes. Drain. Peel and devein shrimp under cold water. Alternate shrimp, onions and bay leaves in a shallow baking dish.

Combine remaining ingredients and mix well. Pour over shrimp. Cover and refrigerate overnight.

Serves six.

PICKLED SHRIMP

2 pounds cooked shrimp, shelled
1 onion, sliced, and separate into rings
1/4 cup black olives, pitted
1/4 cup pimiento stuffed green olives
1 lemon, sliced
1/4 cup cider vinegar
1/2 cup vegetable oil
1/4 cup lemon juice
1/4 cup parsley, chopped
1 tablespoon Dijon style mustard
1 bay leaf
1/4 teaspoon garlic powder
1 tablespoon fresh basil
1/4 teaspoon fresh ground black pepper

Mix shrimp, onion, olives and lemon in a bowl. Combine remaining ingredients in another bowl and mix. Pour over shrimp. Cover and marinate overnight. Serve chilled.

Serves six.

POTTED SHRIMP

3/4 pound cooked shrimp, shelled
juice of one lemon
pinch of cayenne
4 tablespoons clarified butter
4 tablespoons butter
salt to taste
fresh ground pepper to taste

Mix shrimp with lemon juice, cayenne, salt and pepper. Pack into four small oven ramekins. Top each with one tablespoon butter. Bake for ten minutes at 350 degrees. Remove ramekins from over and pour in one tablespoon of clarified butter. Cool.

Serves four.

QUICK SHRIMP QUICHE

1 pound raw shrimp, shelled and deveined
1 package refrigerated crescent dinner rolls
12 very shin slices pepperoni, shredded
2 tablespoons butter
1 pimiento, slivered
1 1/2 cups Swiss cheese, grated
4 eggs
1 3/4 cups light cream
pinch of salt
pinch of pepper
pinch dry mustard

Grease a 13x9x2 inch baking dish and cover bottom and sides with crescent rolls. Press firmly to seal all seams.

Sauté shrimp and pepperoni in butter. Add pimiento. Sprinkle cheese on crescent dough crust. Top with shrimp mixture. Beat eggs with remaining ingredients. Pour over filling in crust.

Bake at 400 degrees for 10 minutes. Reduce heat to 325 degrees and bake for 30 minutes.

Makes 24 appetizers.

SEAFOOD AND CHEESE SPREAD

1 (4 1/2-ounce) can shrimp, drained
1 (4-ounce) can crab, drained, flaked and
    cartilage removed
1/4 cup mayonnaise
2 tablespoons lemon juice
16 ounces whipped cream cheese
dash garlic powder
2 tablespoons chives, chopped
2/3 cup celery, chopped
2 tablespoons sweet pickle relish
3/4 cup chili sauce
1 teaspoon Worcestershire sauce
1/4 cup fresh parsley, chopped

Beat mayonnaise, lemon juice, cream cheese, garlic and Worcestershire sauce until smooth. Spread and flatten into a nine inch circle on a plate.

Combine relish, celery, chives and chili sauce and spread on top of the cheese mixture. Arrange crab and shrimp on top. Sprinkle with chopped parsley. Serve with crackers.

Serves 18-20.

SHRIMP AND ANCHOVY BUTTER

1 pound raw shrimp, shelled and butterflied
12 ounces beer, de carbonated
1/4 cup pickling spices
6 tablespoons butter
1/2 teaspoon anchovy paste

Put flat beer and pickling spices in a pan and boil. Add shrimp and cook five minutes. Leave shrimp in liquid and refrigerate for one hour. Drain and chill.

Melt butter in a saucepan and stir in anchovy paste to taste. Place mixture in a bowl for dipping. Serve with chilled shrimp.

Serves two to four.

SHRIMP AND ARTICHOKE DIP

1 pound cooked shrimp, shelled and chopped
1 (14-ounce) can artichoke hearts, rinsed,
**   drained, and chopped**
1 medium onion, chopped
1 cup sour cream
1 cup mayonnaise
1/4 cup chili sauce
1 tablespoon Worcestershire sauce
1 drop hot pepper sauce

Combine all ingredients and chill over night.
Makes four cups.

SHRIMP AND CHILI SAUCE

2 cups raw shrimp, shelled and deveined
1/4 cup butter
1 clove garlic, minced
1 teaspoon dried dillweed
1 cup chili sauce

Melt butter and sauté garlic in a hot skillet. Add dillweed and shrimp. Cook, stirring frequently, until shrimp are done. Serve with chili sauce.
Serves two.

SHRIMP BALLS

1 1/2 pounds raw shrimp shelled and minced
1 medium onion, grated
1 medium potato, grated
1 egg
pepper to taste
salt to taste
oil for deep frying

Combine all ingredients to form a thick batter. Drop by spoon into hot oil. Fry until golden brown. Drain. Serve hot with cocktail sauce.
Serves six.

SHRIMP BUTTER

1/2 cup shrimp, shelled
8 tablespoons butter

Melt butter and stir in shrimp. Cook until shrimp turn pink. Add to a blender and process until shrimp are creamy. Spread on bread. Toast in the oven.

Makes one cup.

SHRIMP CANAPÉS

2 cups cooked shrimp, shelled and chopped
1 large cucumber
1/2 cup mayonnaise
1 tablespoon lemon juice
2 teaspoons onion, finely chopped
1/4 teaspoon salt
16 slices bread
fresh parsley for garnish

Wash and cut cucumber in half lengthwise. With a spoon, scoop out seeds from center of each section. Chop one cup cucumber. Save the remaining cucumber to slice and use for garnish. Combine chopped cucumber with remaining ingredients. Chill.

Trim crusts from bread and toast. Spread shrimp mixture on toast. Cut toast into fourths. Garnish with parsley and cucumber slices.

Make sixty four small sandwiches.

SHRIMP CHILI PASTE

1/2 cup cooked shrimp, shelled
2 tablespoons chili sauce
2 tablespoons mayonnaise
2 tablespoons lemon juice
1/4 teaspoon dillweed

Blend ingredients until smooth. Serve with crackers or toast.

Makes 3/4 cup.

SHRIMP COCKTAIL

2 pounds cooked shrimp, cleaned, shelled and chilled
1/2 cup olive oil
1 tablespoon horseradish
3 tablespoons paprika
1 tablespoon prepared mustard
1 teaspoon celery seed
1/4 teaspoon pepper
1/4 teaspoon onion powder
1/4 cup vinegar

Arrange shrimp in six serving dishes. Mix remaining ingredients. Chill and serve with shrimp.

Serves six.

SHRIMP CANAPÉS WITH SHARP CHEESE

8 ounces shrimp, shelled and chopped
8 tablespoons butter.
8 ounces sharp cheese, grated
2 tablespoons mayonnaise
1/2 teaspoon salt
1/2 teaspoon garlic salt
6 English muffins

Mix all ingredients except muffins in a mixer. Cut muffins into fourths. Spread mixture on muffins. Freeze for 30 minutes.

Arrange on a cookie sheet and broil until bubbly and golden brown.

Serves four.

SHRIMP DIP

1 (4 1/4 ounce) can shrimp, drained
3 ounces cream cheese
1/4 cup mayonnaise
1 cup sour cream
1/2 cup cocktail sauce
2 tablespoons green onion, chopped
1 teaspoon lemon juice

Beat cheese and mayonnaise until smooth. Stir in remaining ingredients. Chill. Serve with assorted fresh vegetables or cracker.
Makes 2 1/2 cups.

SHRIMP DIP WITH CREAMED CHEESE AND CHIVES

1 1/2 pounds cooked shrimp, shelled and chopped
16 ounces whipped cream cheese
1 tablespoon Worcestershire sauce
1 1/2 teaspoons hot pepper sauce
1 cup mayonnaise
2 tablespoons chives, chopped

Combine all ingredients. Chill for several hours.
Makes three cups.

SHRIMP DIP WITH ONION

1/2 pound cooked shrimp, shelled and chopped
2 cups sour cream
1/4 cup chili sauce
1 package dry onion soup mix
1 tablespoon parsley, chopped

Combine ingredients. Mix and chill.
Garnish with parsley.
Makes three cups.

SHRIMP EGG ROLLS

2 cups cooked shrimp, shelled and chopped
2 cups Romaine lettuce, shredded
1 clove garlic, minced
1 large onion, chopped
1/2 cup snow peas, chopped
1/2 cup water chestnuts, drained and chopped
2 cups fresh bean sprouts
2 tablespoons oil
1 egg, beaten
2 tablespoons dry sherry
1 tablespoon soy sauce
1/8 teaspoon cayenne pepper
10 egg roll wrappers
sweet and sour dipping sauce
hot mustard dipping sauce

Sauté garlic and onion in oil. Add lettuce, peas, chestnuts and sprouts. Stir fry about three minutes. Cover and steam one minute. In a large bowl, combine vegetables, shrimp, egg, sherry, soy sauce and pepper.

Spoon one half cup of the filling into the center of each wrapper. Fold one long side of the wrapper over the top and around the filling. Fold in both ends and compress filling into wrapper. Fold remaining side up and over the tip and ends. Brush rolls with oil. Place rolls, seam side down on baking sheet making sure they are not touching.

Bake at 350 degrees for 15 minutes or until golden brown. Serve with dipping sauces.

Serves four.

SHRIMP FRITTERS

1 cup cooked shrimp, shelled and chopped
4 eggs, separated
1/2 teaspoon celery salt
1 tablespoon parsley, chopped
2 tablespoons flour
oil for frying

2 tablespoons olive oil
1 (10-ounce) can tomatoes and green chilies
1 onion, chopped
1 garlic clove, minced
1/4 teaspoon pepper

Beat eggs yolks with celery salt, parsley and flour. Beat egg whites until stiff and fold into egg yolk mixture. Add shrimp. Drop by spoon into hot oil and deep fry until golden. Drain and serve hot.

Prepare sauce by sautéing onion and garlic with olive oil in a skillet. Add tomatoes, chilies and pepper and bring to a boil. Reduce heat and simmer, covered, for 20 minutes. Serve with fritters.

APPETIZERS

SHRIMP IN GARLIC MAYONNAISE

1 1/2 pounds cooked shrimp, shelled
4 cloves garlic, minced finely
2 egg yolks
1 cup olive oil
juice of one lemon
1 teaspoon water
1/4 cup parsley, minced
salt to taste
pepper to taste

In a blender, combine garlic and eggs yolks. Slowly add half of oil until the sauce thickens. Add lemon juice and water. Add the rest of the oil until blended. Add salt, pepper and parsley and blend. Serve with chilled shrimp.

Serves two to four.

# SHRIMP

SHRIMP MUSHROOM DIP

2 1/2 pounds raw shrimp shelled and chopped
2 cups green onions, chopped
1/2 cup green pepper, chopped
1/2 cup celery, chopped
1 small jar pimientos, drained and chopped
2 tablespoons butter
2 cans cream of mushroom soup
garlic powder to taste
cayenne pepper to taste

Sauté onions, green pepper, celery, and pimientos in butter. Add shrimp and cook about one minute. Add soup and simmer eight to ten minutes. Season to taste with garlic powder and pepper.

Makes four to five cups.

SHRIMP PACIFIC

1 1/2 pounds raw shrimp, shelled
2 oranges, peeled, sectioned and halved
1 cup frozen small whole onions, thawed
1 tomato, peeled, seeded, cut into 8 wedges and halved
3/4 cup vinegar
1/3 cup salad oil
1/3 cup lemon juice
1/3 cup catsup
1 tablespoon capers
1 tablespoon parsley, snipped
1 clove garlic, crushed
1 teaspoon sugar
1 teaspoon mustard seed
1/2 teaspoon celery seed
1/4 teaspoon pepper

Cook shrimp uncovered in salted water for one to three minutes. Drain.

Combine shrimp, oranges, and tomato. Mix vinegar, oil, lemon juice, catsup, capers, parsley, garlic, sugar, mustard, and pepper. Pour over shrimp. Cover and marinate in refrigerator overnight.

Makes five and one half cups.

SHRIMP PARMESAN

1 pound raw shrimp, shelled and deveined
1 teaspoon chives, chopped
1 clove garlic, minced
1/4 cup butter
2 tablespoons dry sherry
3 tablespoons grated parmesan cheese

Melt butter in a skillet. Sauté chives and garlic until soft. Add shrimp and sauté over medium heat for two minutes. Add sherry. Top with cheese.
Serves eight.

SHRIMP PASTE

2 (4 1/2-ounce) cans of shrimp
1/2 cup butter
2 tablespoons dry sherry
1 tablespoon onion, grated
1/4 teaspoon mace
1 tablespoon lemon juice
1/4 teaspoon dry mustard
1/4 teaspoon cayenne pepper

Grind shrimp in a food processor. Cream butter and beat in sherry, mace, lemon juice, mustard, pepper and onion. Add shrimp and beat until smooth. Serve with crackers or toast.
Makes two cups.

SHRIMP PATE

1 pound cooked shrimp, shelled
3 tablespoons lemon juice
1/2 teaspoon mace
dash of Tabasco sauce
1 teaspoon prepared mustard
1/2 cup soft butter
fresh ground pepper and salt to taste

Blend shrimp, lemon juice, mace, mustard and Tabasco until mixture is coarsely blended. Stir mixture into butter. Add salt and pepper to taste. Serve with crackers or toast.

Makes two cups.

SHRIMP PUFFS

1 cup cooked shrimp, chopped
1/2 cup flour
1 egg
1 tablespoon soy sauce
1/2 cup milk
oil for deep frying

Make a batter of flour, egg, soy sauce and milk. Stir in shrimp. Drop a tablespoon of mixture into hot oil. Deep fry until golden brown. Drain.

Serves two.

SHRIMP WITH AVOCADOS

1 pound cooked shrimp, cut in half
2 avocados
2 tablespoons lemon juice
6 tablespoons olive oil
1 teaspoon dry mustard
salt to taste
pepper to taste
fresh parsley for garnish

Cut avocados in half lengthwise and remove the stones. Brush with lemon juice. Around the center drape shrimp halves. Mix remaining ingredients together and fill the center of the avocados. Garnish with parsley.

Serves four.

SHRIMP WITH CUCUMBER DIPPING SAUCE

1 pound cooked shrimp, shelled
1 cup fresh lime juice
2 tablespoons green pepper, minced
2 tablespoons onion, chopped
1 cucumber peeled, seeded and chopped
1/2 cup tomato juice
pepper to taste
hot pepper sauce to taste

Combine shrimp and lime juice and marinate one hour in refrigerator. Drain shrimp, reserving the juice. To make sauce, combine juice with remaining ingredients.

Serves four.

SHRIMP WON TON

1/2 pound raw shrimp, shelled
1 raw pork chop, cut into small strips
2 green onions, minced
2 large mushrooms, mined
1 teaspoon cilantro, minced
4 water chestnuts, minced
1 tablespoon soy sauce
1 tablespoon dry sherry
1/4 teaspoon sugar
1/4 teaspoon salt
dash of pepper
1 teaspoon cornstarch
1 egg white
1 package won ton skins
chili sauce and hot mustard for dipping

Grind or puree pork and shrimp. Mix vegetables with meat mixture. Add soy sauce, sherry, seasonings, cornstarch and egg white. Mix thoroughly.

Place a teaspoon of filling in the center of each won ton skin. Slightly moisten the edges of the skin with water. Fold each skin in half, making a triangle. Pinch the seams together, then fold the points inward, bringing them almost together.

Deep fry five to six won ton in hot oil until golden brown.

Serve with chili sauce and mustard.

Serves two.

SPICY POTTED SHRIMP

8 ounces medium shrimp, shelled and coarsely chopped
1 tablespoon chives, chopped
3/4 teaspoon salt
1/2 small fresh chili pepper, minced
1/2 teaspoon lemon grated
dash of Tabasco sauce
5 tablespoons clarified butter

Melt butter in medium skillet over low heat. Stir in chives, salt, chili pepper and lemon. Cook tow minutes. Add shrimp and cook over low heat for three minutes. Add Tabasco. Puree coarsely in a food processor. Pack mixture into a small bowl. Cover with plastic wrap and chill for four hours. Serve with toast.

Makes 1 1/4 cup.

TOMATO SHRIMP DIP

2 cups cooked shrimp, chopped
1/2 cup water
1 envelop Knox gelatin
1 can tomato soup, undiluted
1/2 cup green peppers, chopped
1/2 cup onion, chopped
1 (8 ounce) package cream cheese
1 cup mayonnaise

Mix water and gelatin. Set aside. Heat soup. Stir in water and gelatin mixture. Add remaining ingredients and mix until smooth. Refrigerate until set.

Makes three cups.

VALDEZ MARINATED SHRIMP

3 pounds cooked shrimp, shelled
1 1/4 cups vegetable oil
1/3 cup vinegar
1/2 cup catsup
2 teaspoons sugar
3 teaspoons Worcestershire sauce
2 cloves garlic
2 teaspoons dry mustard
1/4 teaspoon pepper
1/8 teaspoon hot pepper sauce
1 large onion, sliced thin and separated into rings
4 bay leaves

Combine all ingredients, except shrimp, onion and bay leaves, in a food processor and blend until smooth. Add shrimp, onions and bay leaves. Refrigerate and marinate two days. Serve cold.

Serves twelve.

AUSTIN'S PESTO SHRIMP AND PASTA SALAD

1/2 pound cooked shrimp, shelled and deveined
8 ounces fusilli or rotelle pasta
1/2 cup red bell pepper, thinly sliced
1/2 cup yellow bell pepper, thinly sliced
1/2 cup green bell pepper, thinly sliced
2/3 cup pesto sauce
fresh basil for garnish

Cook pasta per package instructions and rinse under cold water. Cut shrimp in half lengthwise. Combine shrimp, peppers and pasta in a large bowl. Add pesto sauce and toss to coat. Garnish with basil.

Serves two.

SHRIMP TARTS

2 cups cooked shrimp, shelled and chopped
3/4 cup celery, chopped
1/4 cup green onions, finely chopped
1 medium apple, cored and chopped
1 cup seedless grapes, halved
1/2 cup pecans, coarsely chopped
1/4 cup sour cream
1/4 cup mayonnaise
4 teaspoons lemon juice
1/8 teaspoon dry mustard
2 cups flour
1 teaspoon salt
1/2 cup salad oil
1 cup Cheddar cheese, grated
3 tablespoons cold water

In a medium bowl, combine first six ingredients. In a small bowl mix, sour cream, mayonnaise, lemon juice and mustard. Fold into shrimp mixture. Chill.

Combine flour and salt. Stir in salad oil with a fork. Stir in cheese and blend until mixture resembles coarse crumbs. Stir in water, gathering dough to a ball. Roll dough between pieces of wax paper and cut in circles to fit muffin pans. Bake a 425 degrees about 12 minutes. Remove from pans and cool.

Fill with shrimp mixture.

Serves five.

SHRIMP IN CHEESE TARTS

2 cups cooked shrimp, shelled and chopped
3/4 cup celery, chopped
1/4 cup green onions, finely chopped
1 medium apple, cored and chopped
1 cup seedless grapes, halved
1/2 cup pecans, coarsely chopped
1/4 cup sour cream
1/4 cup mayonnaise
4 teaspoons lemon juice
1/8 teaspoon dry mustard
2 cups flour
1 teaspoon salt
1/2 cup salad oil
1 cup Cheddar cheese, grated
3 tablespoons cold water

In a medium bowl, combine shrimp, celery, onions, apple, grapes and pecans. In a small bowl mix, sour cream, mayonnaise, lemon juice and mustard. Fold into shrimp mixture Chill.

Combine flour and salt. Stir in salad oil with a fork. Stir in cheese and blend until mixture resembles coarse crumbs. Stir in water, gathering dough to a boil. Roll half dough between pieces of wax paper and cut in circles to fit muffin pans. Bake a 425 degrees about 12 minutes. Remove from pans and cool.

Fill with shrimp mixture.
Serves five.

CORDOVA SHRIMP

2 cups cooked shrimp, shelled and deveined
1/4 cup wine vinegar
1/4 cup vegetable oil
2 tablespoons sugar
1/4 cup long grain rice
2 cups boiling water
1/4 teaspoon salt
1 cup fresh pea pods, sliced in one inch pieces
1 green onion, sliced
fresh spinach
1/4 cup toasted almonds, sliced

Combine shrimp, vinegar, oil and sugar. Chill and marinate four hours. Cook rice in boiling water and salt for 15 minutes. Remove from heat and cool slightly. Stir in pea pods and onions. Chill. Drain shrimp, reserving marinate. Arrange spinach on four salad plates. Top with rice mixture and pour marinade over rice. Garnish with almonds.
Serves four.

CREAMY SHRIMP SALAD

3 pounds cooked shrimp, shelled and deveined
4 hard boiled eggs, yolks sieved and whites chopped
3 tablespoons sugar
4 tablespoons white wine vinegar
2 teaspoons Dijon style mustard
1/4 teaspoon black pepper
2 cups mayonnaise
1 tablespoon capers, drained
2 onions, thinly sliced
1/4 cup whipped cream
1/2 cup sour cream
lettuce leaves

Combine egg yolks, sugar, vinegar, mustard, pepper and mayonnaise. Stir in capers, egg whites, onions and shrimp. Fold in whipped and sour cream. Serve over lettuce.
Serves eight.

CURRIED SHRIMP SALAD

1 (4 1/2 ounces) can shrimp, rinsed and drained
1/2 cup mayonnaise
1 tablespoon soy sauce
1 teaspoon lemon juice
1/2 cup fresh bean sprouts
1/2 cup celery, chopped
1 teaspoon curry powder
lettuce leaves

　　Combine ingredients except lettuce leaves. Chill. Serve on
lettuce leaves.
　　Serves two.

SHRIMP

DILLED SHRIMP

1 1/2 pounds cooked shrimp, shelled and deveined
1/2 cup cucumber, peeled and chopped
1/2 cup mayonnaise
1/2 cup sour cream
2 tablespoons onion, minced
1 tablespoon dillweed
2 teaspoons lemon juice
1 clove garlic, minced
8 drops hot pepper sauce
salt to taste
pepper to taste
lettuce

Combine cucumber, mayonnaise, sour cream, onion, dill weed, lemon juice, garlic, pepper sauce, salt and pepper. Mix well. Fold in shrimp. Arrange over lettuce.
Serves six.

GRAPEFRUIT AND SHRIMP SALAD

1/2 pound raw shrimp, shelled
3 tablespoons onion, chopped fine
2 teaspoons lemon juice
2 teaspoons dry white wine
1/3 cup olive oil
1/3 cup parsley, chopped
4 grapefruit, peeled and divided into segments
1 1/4 cup mayonnaise
6 drops Tabasco sauce
salt to taste
pepper to taste
pinch of paprika
pitted black olives for garnish
small tomatoes for garnish
lettuce leaves for garnish

Combine shrimp, onion, parsley, lemon, wine, oil, salt and pepper. Heat until sizzling. Set aside to cool.

Drain shrimp. Combine with grapefruit and fold in mayonnaise and Tabasco. Serve chilled with lettuce leaves. Sprinkle with paprika. Garnish with olives and tomatoes.

Serves six.

HALIBUT COVE SHRIMP

1 1/2 pounds cooked shrimp, shelled and deveined
1/2 pound fresh mushrooms, sliced
1 cup fresh bean sprouts
1 cup alfalfa sprouts
4 green onions, sliced
1 small green pepper, thinly sliced
1 can (eight ounce) water chestnuts, drained and sliced
1/4 cup teriyaki sauce
3 tablespoons sesame seed oil
2 tablespoons rice wine vinegar
1/2 teaspoon ground ginger
1 teaspoon sesame seeds
leaf lettuce

Carefully mix first seven ingredients. Combine teriyaki sauce, oil, vinegar and ginger. Pour over shrimp mixture. Cover and refrigerate two hours. Arrange lettuce on plates Mound shrimp mixture on top of the lettuce. Sprinkle with sesame seeds and serve.

Serves four.

HOT SHRIMP SALAD

1/2 pound cooked shrimp, shelled and sliced
2 cups cooked rice
2 tablespoons chili sauce
2 tablespoons vinegar
1 teaspoon sugar
1 tablespoon horseradish
1/4 cup oil
2 tablespoons parsley, chopped
toasted almonds for garnish

Combine chili sauce, vinegar, sugar, horseradish and oil. Heat. Add shrimp and rice. Heat again. Sprinkle with parsley and almonds.

Serves two.

MARINATED ORANGE SHRIMP

1 1/2 pounds cooked shrimp, shelled and deveined
2 large oranges, peeled and sliced thin
1 small onion, sliced and separated into rings
1/3 cup cider vinegar
1/3 cup fresh lemon juice
1/4 cup sugar
1 cup oil
1 tablespoon paprika
2 teaspoons dry mustard
2 cloves garlic, minced
1/2 teaspoon salt
1/4 teaspoon crushed red chilies

Layer cooled shrimp with oranges and onion rings in a glass serving bowl. Combine remaining ingredients. Pour over shrimp. Cover and refrigerate one hour.

Serves four to six.

MARINATED SHRIMP SALAD

**4 cups cooked shrimp, shelled and deveined
1/4 teaspoon paprika
bottle of French dressing
1/3 cup mayonnaise
16 small sweet pickles
shredded lettuce**

Sprinkle paprika over shrimp and then cover with French dressing. Chill and marinate for one hour. Stir in mayonnaise and arrange shrimp over lettuce. Garnish with pickles.
Serves eight.

ORANGE SHRIMP SALAD

1 pound cooked shrimp, shelled and deveined
3 large oranges, sectioned
1 medium red onion, sliced thinly
1/2 pound fresh spinach, torn into bite size pieces
3/4 cup olive oil
1/4 cup fresh lemon juice
1 teaspoon sugar
1 teaspoon prepared Dijon mustard
salt to taste
pepper to taste

Arrange spinach on a large serving plate. Arrange shrimp, orange sections and onions on top of spinach. Make a dressing of oil, lemon juice, sugar, mustard, salt and pepper. Pour over chilled salad.

Serves four.

QUICK SHRIMP SALAD

**1 pound cooked shrimp, shelled and deveined
1 hard boiled egg, chopped
1/2 cup mayonnaise
1 tablespoon sweet pickle relish
2 tablespoons onion, minced
2 tablespoons green pepper, finely chopped
dash hot pepper sauce
salt to taste
pepper to taste
lettuce leaves**

Combine ingredients. Serve on leaf lettuce.
Serves four.

SEAFOOD SALAD

2 pieces lobster claw meat, cooked and flaked
20 medium cooked shrimp, shelled and deveined
1 tablespoon garlic butter
1 ounce of raw fish, sliced and cooked
2 ounces of tuna, raw cut into 1/4 inch cubes
5 pieces asparagus tips
11 pieces small green beans
1 ounce avocado
1 ounce papaya
1 ounce mixed salad greens
2 ounces tarragon vinaigrette
4 spears chives, cut one inch long
5 springs chervil
olive oil for sautéing
butter for sautéing
salt to taste
pepper to taste

Sauté shrimp in olive oil until cooked. Add lobster meat and melt in garlic butter. In a mixing bowl, place shrimp, lobster and remainder of ingredients. Season salad with salt and pepper. Toss salad and garnish.

Serves one.

SHRIMP AND CHEESE SALAD

1 pound cooked shrimp, shelled and deveined
1 cup mild Cheddar cheese, grated
2 tomatoes, cut in bite size pieces
1 1/2 quarts leaf lettuce
1/4 cup green onions, sliced
1/2 cup sliced ripe olives
1 cup cucumber, sliced
3/4 cup creamy Italian salad dressing

Combine first seven ingredients in large salad bowl. Toss with salad dressing.

Serves six.

SHRIMP AND PASTA SALAD

4 (4 1/2 ounce) cans shrimp, drained
2 cups cooked macaroni shells
1/2 cup raw cauliflower, chopped
1/2 cup raw broccoli, chopped
1 cup celery, sliced
1 tablespoon pimento, chopped
1/2 cup mayonnaise
1/4 cut sweet pickle relish
1/4 cup parsley, chopped
1/2 cup mayonnaise
1/4 cup sour cream
3 tablespoons French dressing
1 tablespoon lemon juice
1 tablespoon onion, minced
1/2 teaspoon celery seed
1/2 teaspoon salt
pepper to taste
1 hard cooked egg, chopped for garnish
lettuce leaves

Combine shrimp, shells, cauliflower, broccoli, celery, relish and pimento. Mix together mayonnaise, sour cream French dressing, lemon juice, onion celery seed, salt and pepper. Fold into shrimp mixture to coat shrimp and vegetables well. Serve on lettuce lined plates. Garnish with chopped egg.
Serves six.

SHRIMP AND PEA SALAD

1 (4 1/2 ounce) can shrimp, drained
2 cups cooked peas
1/3 cup ripe olives, pitted and sliced
1/3 cup salad oil
3 tablespoons vinegar
1/2 teaspoon salt
1/8 teaspoon dried dillweed, crushed
dash of pepper
3 to 4 cups torn lettuce
2 hard boiled eggs, sliced

Combine peas, shrimp and olives. Combine oil, vinegar, salt, dillweed and pepper. Mix well. Pour over shrimp. Cover and refrigerate several hours. Arrange lettuce in a salad bowl. Top with shrimp mixture. Toss with dressing. Garnish salad with egg slices.

Serves four.

SHRIMP AND SPINACH SALAD

1 pound cooked shrimp, shelled and deveined
2 1/2 tablespoons tarragon vinegar
1 tablespoon Dijon mustard
3 large cloves garlic, pressed
3/4 cup olive oil
2 medium fennel bulbs, cored and cut into strips
4 1/2 tablespoons fresh chives, chopped
salt to taste
pepper to taste
2 large bunches fresh spinach leaves, stemmed

Mix vinegar, mustard and garlic in medium bowl. Gradually whisk in oil. Add shrimp, fennel and three table-spoons chives; toss well. Season with salt. Cover and let stand 30 minutes at room temperature.

Arrange spinach leaves on six plates. Tear remaining spinach into bite size pieces. Toss with shrimp. Mound salad on plates. Season with pepper. Garnish with chives.

Serves six.

SHRIMP AVOCADO SALAD

12 to 15 large cooked shrimp, unshelled
3/4 cup mayonnaise
2 teaspoons mustard seeds
1/4 teaspoon ground cumin
1/4 teaspoon curry powder
1 large head of endive
large avocado, peeled and sliced

Combine mayonnaise, mustard seeds, cumin and curry powder. Arrange avocado, shrimp and endive on each plate along with dipping sauce.

Serves three.

SHRIMP AVOCADO SALAD WITH PISTACHIO NUTS

12 large cooked shrimp, shelled, deveined and chopped
1/4 cup salad oil
1/4 cup white wine vinegar
4 large cloves garlic, minced
2 medium avocados
4 to 8 large butter lettuce leaves, washed and crisped
2 tablespoons pistachio nuts, roasted and
    coarsely chopped

Combine oil, vinegar and garlic. Add shrimp to oil mixture. Stir to coat. Set aside.

Cut avocados in half lengthwise and remove pits. With a spoon remove avocado from shells in bite-size chunks. Add avocado chunks to the shrimp mixture and stir to coat.

To serve, line four salad plates with lettuce. Fill avocado shells with salad mixture and set on each plate. Sprinkle with pistachios.

Serves four.

SHRIMP CANTALOUPE SALAD

10 large cooked shrimp, shelled and deveined
1/4 cantaloupe, peeled and cut in wedges
6 green grapes, halved
mayonnaise flavored with curry to taste
lettuce leaves

Place cantaloupe wedge on bed of lettuce. Arrange shrimp on top of wedge. Cover with curried mayonnaise. Garnish with grapes.
Serves one.

SHRIMP FRUIT SALAD

1 (4 1/2 ounce) can shrimp, drained
2 medium bananas, sliced
2 tomatoes cut in wedges
1 can mandarin orange sections, drained
1 cup seedless grapes
2 tablespoons oil
2 tablespoons cider vinegar
1/8 teaspoon black pepper
1 teaspoon honey
2 tablespoons onion, grated
ripe olives, pitted and sliced for garnish

Combine shrimp and fruit in serving bowl. Mix remaining ingredients. Pour over shrimp. Add olive slices for garnish.
Serves four.

SHRIMP GELATIN SALAD

1 pound cooked shrimp, shelled and deveined
1/2 cup cold water
2 one-tablespoon envelopes unflavored gelatin
1 cup mayonnaise
1/4 cup green olives, sliced
2 teaspoons horseradish
2 teaspoons onion, minced
1/4 cup lemon juice
1/4 teaspoon paprika
1 cup sour cream

Combine water and gelatin to soften. Stir in mayonnaise. Add remaining ingredients. Turn into gelatin mold and chill until congealed.

Serves six.

SHRIMP IN TOMATO ASPIC RING

1 pound medium cooked shrimp, shelled and deveined
2 tablespoons gelatin
2 cups tomato juice
2 teaspoons fresh onion, grated
2 tablespoons sweet pickles, chopped
1 tablespoon lemon juice
2 teaspoons horseradish
1/4 teaspoon salt
black pepper to taste
lettuce leaves
mayonnaise for garnish

Soften gelatin in 1/2 cup of tomato juice for five minutes. Scald remaining tomato juice and stir into gelatin until gelatin is dissolved. Add the next six ingredients. Stir in shrimp. Turn into a ring mold and chill until firm. Unmold onto a bed of lettuce leaves and garnish with mayonnaise.

Serves six.

SHRIMP LOUIS

4 cup cooked shrimp, shelled and deveined
1 quart iceberg lettuce, shredded
2 tomatoes, quartered
12 black olives, pitted
1 green pepper, sliced into rings
2 cup chick peas
leaf lettuce for garnish
1 1/2 cups chili sauce
1 cup mayonnaise
1/4 cup green pepper, chopped
1/2 teaspoon dry mustard
1 tablespoon onion, minced
1 tablespoon pimento, chopped
1/2 teaspoon horseradish
dash hot pepper
fresh ground pepper to taste

Arrange lettuce leaves on four plates. Divide iceberg lettuce between the four plates. Arrange shrimp over lettuce. Garnish with tomatoes, olives, pepper and peas.

Combine remaining ingredients and mix well. Pour over shrimp and vegetables.

Serves four.

SHRIMP MEDLEY

3/4 pounds cooked shrimp, shelled and deveined
1 large seedless orange, peeled, sliced and cut in quarters
1 cup purple grapes, sliced in half and seeded
1 small can white asparagus tips
leaf lettuce
1/4 cup mayonnaise
1/4 cup sour cream
1 teaspoon chili sauce
1 tablespoon lemon juice
1/8 teaspoon Worcestershire sauce
1 teaspoon horseradish, grated
4 cooked crab claws for garnish
whole purple grapes for garnish
orange slices for garnish

Arrange lettuce on four plates. Arrange orange sections, grape halves, shrimp and asparagus on lettuce.

Combine mayonnaise, sour cream. chili sauce, lemon juice, Worcestershire sauce and horseradish. Mix until smooth. Pour dressing over shrimp on plates. Garnish each plate with crab, grapes and orange slices.

Serves four.

SHRIMP PASTA SALAD

1 pound raw shrimp, shelled, cleaned and deveined
2 cups zucchini, thinly sliced
2 cups fresh mushrooms, sliced
1 cup green beans, cut into one inch lengths
2 tablespoons oil
8 ounces rotelle or corkscrew pasta, cooked according to package instructions
2 tablespoons lemon juice
1 medium onion, thinly sliced and separated into rings
1 clove garlic, minced
3/4 cup Italian dressing
lettuce leaves

Sauté zucchini, mushrooms and green beans in oil until they soften slightly. Remove from pan. Add shrimp, lemon juice, garlic and onion. Sauté until shrimp turn pink. Remove to bowl of vegetables. Add pasta and dressing, tossing to coat. Chill. Serve over lettuce leaves.

Serves eight.

SHRIMP RICE SALAD

3 (4 1/2 ounce) cans shrimp, drained
2 cups cooked brown rice
1/2 cup fresh parsley, chopped
3/4 cup celery, sliced thin
1/4 cup ripe olives, sliced
1/2 cup mayonnaise
2 tablespoons French dressing
2 tablespoons lemon juice
1/2 teaspoon curry powder
lettuce leaves

Combine rice, parsley, celery, olives and shrimp. Mix mayonnaise with French dressing, lemon juice, and curry. Mix until smooth. Fold into shrimp mixture and serve on lettuce leaves.
Serves six.

SHRIMP, RICE AND BROCCOLI SALAD

1/2 pound cooked shrimp, shelled and deveined
1/4 cup rice vinegar
2 tablespoons sesame seed oil
2 tablespoons vegetable oil
1 1/2 tablespoon soy sauce
1 tablespoon fresh ginger, peeled and minced
2 1/2 cups cooked rice, cooled
2 cups cooked broccoli florets
1 red bell pepper, seeded and coarsely chopped

Mix sesame oil, vegetable oil, vinegar, soy sauce and ginger. Combine rice, broccoli and pepper. Toss with half of dressing. Divide rice mixture between two plates. Put shrimp on top of rice and drizzle with remaining dressing.

Serves two.

SHRIMP SALAD

1 cup cooked shrimp, shelled and chopped into
**   large pieces**
1/2 cup mayonnaise
2 tablespoons onion, minced
1/8 cup chili sauce
1/2 avocado, diced
1/4 cup celery, sliced thin
2 springs fresh dill
salt to taste
pepper to taste

Mix mayonnaise, onion and chili sauce in a large bowl. Add shrimp, avocado and celery Toss lightly. Snip dill into the bowl and season with salt and pepper. Serve on lettuce. Serves two.

SHRIMP SALAD WITH CAPERS

1 1/2 pound raw shrimp
2 tablespoons mixed pickling spices
1 tablespoon parsley
1 bay leaf
3 tablespoons cider vinegar
1 tablespoon salt
1 stalk celery
6 cups boiling water
1/4 cup tarragon vinegar
3 hard boiled eggs, coarsely chopped
1/4 cup mayonnaise
1 cup celery, chopped
1 tablespoon onion, minced
1 tablespoon capers, drained
fresh ground pepper to taste

Add the first seven ingredients to boiling water. Cook shrimp until pink. Drain. Peel and devein shrimp. Sprinkle with tarragon vinegar. Cool for one half hour.

Combine remaining ingredients with shrimp.

Serves six.

SHRIMP SALAD WITH CURRY DRESSING

1 1/2 pounds cooked shrimp, shelled
3 celery stalks, finely diced
1 small onion, finelly chopped
1 teaspoon capers
1 cup mayonnaise
1 tablespoon curry powder
juice of 1/2 lemon
tomato wedges for garnish
cucumber slices for garnish

Mix curry powder, mayonnaise and lemon juice. Add to shrimp, celery, onion and capers. Toss well. Chill.
Serve on a bed of crisp greens with garnishes.
Serves two to four.

SHRIMP SALAD WITH VEGETABLES

1/2 pound cooked shrimp, shelled
1 package of frozen vegetables
1/4 cup French dressing
1 tablespoon pimiento

Cook vegetables according to package instructions. Combine shrimp with vegetables and chill. Add pimiento to dressing and toss with shrimp and vegetable mixture.
Serves six.

SOUTHWEST SHRIMP SALAD

1 1/2 pounds cooked shrimp, shelled and deveined
4 tablespoons lemon juice
1 tablespoon Worcestershire sauce
1/2 teaspoon garlic powder
1/2 teaspoon hot pepper sauce
1/8 teaspoon crushed red chilies
6 corn tortillas, fried
2 avocados, peeled and seeded
2 tablespoons onion, chopped
3 tablespoons mayonnaise
1/2 teaspoon paprika
shredded lettuce for garnish
tomato, chopped for garnish

Combine avocados, onion, lemon juice, mayonnaise, paprika, Worcestershire sauce, garlic powder, hot pepper sauce and chilies. Chill.

Cover each tortilla with some lettuce and avocado mixture. Garnish with more lettuce and tomatoes. Set each tortilla in a bed of lettuce. Arrange shrimp around each.

Serves six.

TABOULEH SEAFOOD SALAD

6 ounces cooked shrimp, shelled and deveined
2 cups warm water
3/4 cup bulgur wheat
1 (ten ounce) can whole baby clams, drained
1 (four ounce) can sliced mushrooms, drained
2 red peppers, cut into 1/2 inch squares
1/4 cup olive oil
2 tablespoons lemon juice
1/2 teaspoon dried dillweed
1/4 teaspoon salt
lettuce leaves for garnish
2 medium tomatoes, sliced and halved
1/2 of a small onion, thinly sliced and separated into rings

In a bowl combine water and bulgur. Let stand for one hour. Drain and press excess water out of bulgur. Combine bulgur, clams, shrimp, mushrooms and pepper.

Combine olive oil, lemon juice, dillweed and salt. Mix well. Pour dressing over salad and toss. Cover and chill. When serving arrange tomatoes and onion rings as garnish.

Serves four.

TROPICAL SHRIMP SALAD

1 1/2 pounds raw shrimp, unshelled
2 tablespoons oil
1 teaspoon ground ginger
1/2 teaspoon curry powder
2 cloves garlic, minced
1/2 cup salad oil
2 tablespoons rum
1/4 cup fresh lime juice
1 tablespoon Dijon-style mustard
1/4 teaspoon salt
dash hot pepper sauce
2 medium papayas, peeled and seeded
3 kiwi fruits, sliced
1 (8 ounce) can sliced pineapple, drained
lime wedges for garnish

    Sauté shrimp in two tablespoons of oil until they turn pink. Drain and cool shrimp. Heat ginger, curry, garlic and oil. Simmer for three minutes. Remove from the heat and cool. To oil mixture add rum, lime juice, mustard, salt and hot pepper. Whisk in one tablespoon of soft papaya. Blend until smooth and creamy. Pour over shelled and deveined shrimp. Cover and marinate at least two hours. Drain shrimp and arrange on serving dish with fruit. Cover with dressing.
    Serves four.

WHITTER SHRIMP SALAD

2 cups cooked shrimp, shelled and deveined
1/2 cup celery, chopped
1/2 cup toasted almonds, slivered
1/2 teaspoon celery salt
1/4 teaspoon white pepper
2 tablespoons lemon juice
1/2 cup mayonnaise
lettuce leaves

Combine ingredients. Chill. Serve on lettuce leaves.
Serves six.

WILTED SPINACH SALAD AND SHRIMP

1 pound cooked shrimp, shelled and deveined
4 cups spinach, washed and drained
1 orange, peeled and sliced
1/4 medium onion, thinly sliced
2 tablespoons olive oil
6 tablespoons unseasoned rice wine vinegar
2 teaspoons Dijon styled mustard
1/4 teaspoon dried mint
1/8 teaspoon dried oregano
2 tablespoons toasted pecans, chopped

Divide spinach, orange, onion and shrimp onto four dinner plates. In a sauce pan, combine vinegar, oil, mustard, mint and oregano. Stir over low heat until warm. Pour over spinach. Garnish with pecans.

Serves four.

ALASKA SEAFOOD STEW

1/2 pound raw shrimp, shelled and deveined
1 pound halibut, cubed
1/2 pound scallops
1/2 pound crab meat
2 (4 1/2 ounce) cans clams, chopped with liquid reserved
1 pound bacon fried, crumbled
1 medium onion, chopped
1 1/2 cups white wine
2 (14 ounce) cans tomatoes, chopped
1 (4 ounce) can mushrooms, drained
salt to taste
pepper to taste
basil to taste

Sauté onion in small amount of bacon drippings. Add white wine, tomatoes, mushrooms and halibut. Simmer one hour.

Add shrimp, scallops, crab and clams. Cover and simmer about 20 minutes. Season.

Serves six.

COLD SHRIMP CHOWDER

2 cups cooked shrimp, shelled, deveined and chopped
1 pound fresh mushrooms, sliced
1 teaspoon salt
1 1/2 cups water
2 green onions, sliced
3 tablespoons butter
1/4 cup flour
2 cups milk
1 cup light cream
dash of pepper
dash of nutmeg

Combine mushrooms, salt and water. Bring to a boil. Reduce heat and cover. Simmer ten minutes.

Sauté onions in butter. Gradually stir in flour until smooth. Blend in mushroom mixture. Stir and cook until smooth and thick. Stir in milk and then cream. Add shrimp and chill thoroughly. Sprinkle with pepper and nutmeg before serving.

Serves six.

CREAM OF SHRIMP SOUP

1 pound raw shrimp, shelled and deveined
1 1/2 quarts water
2/3 cup dry white wine
2 medium yellow onions, peeled and chopped
2 medium garlic cloves, minced
2 tablespoons olive oil
1 tablespoon butter
2 large tomatoes, peeled, cored, seeded and chopped
1/4 cup parsley, minced
1 large bay leaf
5 tablespoons tomato paste
1/4 teaspoon fresh ground pepper
1/4 teaspoon cayenne pepper
1 teaspoon salt
1/2 cup heavy cream

Place shrimp, water and wine in a large pan. Bring to a simmer. Drain at once. Reserve shrimp and water.

Sauté onions and garlic in olive oil and butter five to six minutes. Add tomatoes, two tablespoons of parsley, bay leaf, tomato paste, black and cayenne peppers. Turn to low heat. Cover and simmer for 25 minutes. Add shrimp liquid and simmer uncovered for one hour.

Discard bay leaf from mixture. Blend mixture until smooth. Add half the shrimp and blend again. Add remaining ingredients and heat again over low heat. Garnish with parsley.

Serves six.

CREAMY SHRIMP BISQUE

1 (4 1/2 ounce) can shrimp, drained and chopped
2 (10 3/4 ounce) cans cream of shrimp soup
1 (10 3/4 ounce) can cream of tomato soup
3 cups milk
1/4 cup dry sherry
1/2 cup whipped cream
pepper to taste
dash nutmeg
fresh parsley, chopped

Combine first five ingredients. Heat until smooth.
Serve with a spoonful of whipped cream. Dust with pepper, nutmeg and parsley.
Serves six.

EASY BOUILLABAISSE

1 (4 1/2 ounce) can shrimp, drained
3-4 pounds of fish
1/2 stick butter
1 onion, minced
1 clove garlic, minced
1 bay leaf
2 cloves
1 teaspoon salt
1/2 teaspoon pepper
1 small can of tomatoes
1 can of clams, in shell

Boil fish skin and bones in enough water to cover for 20 minutes. Strain.

Sauté onions and garlic. Brown fish fillets. Add other ingredients and fish stock. Simmer for 15 minutes.

Serves six.

EASY SHRIMP BISQUE

3/4 pounds cooked shrimp, shelled and deveined
1 green onion, chopped
2 tablespoons celery, chopped
1/4 cup butter
2 tablespoons flour
1/4 teaspoon paprika
dash of pepper
dash of nutmeg
4 cups milk
fresh parsley, chopped

Grind shrimp and set aside.

Sauté onion and celery in butter. Blend in flour, paprika, pepper and nutmeg. Stir constantly until thickened and smooth. Gradually add milk, stirring until smooth and thickened slightly. Add shrimp and heat.

Garnish with parsley.

Serves six.

EASY SHRIMP CHOWDER

1 (4 1/2 ounce) can shrimp, drained
1/2 cup onion, finely chopped
1 tablespoon butter
1 (10 1/2 ounce) can cream of celery soup
1 (10 1/2 ounce) can condensed clam chowder
1 1/2 soup cans water
1 tablespoon parsley, snipped

In saucepan, cook onion in butter until tender. Add remaining ingredients. Simmer about five minutes.
Serves six.

FRENCH BOUILLABAISSE

1 dozen large raw shrimp, shelled and deveined
2 pounds fish fillets
1 pound lobster meat
6 small scallops
1/2 cup butter
1 large onion, minced
1 garlic clove, minced
2 cups fish stock
1 large tomato, peeled
1 teaspoon salt
1 lemon, sliced
1/4 cup red wine

Sauté onion in butter. Add garlic and seafood. Sauté about five minutes until seafood is cooked. Add stock and other ingredients and simmer ten minutes. Serve hot with lemon on top.
Serves six.

JAMBALAYA

1 pound cooked shrimp, shelled and deveined
1 ham bone
2 stalks celery
1 carrot
1 small onion, quartered
2 cups ham, chopped
1 medium onion, chopped
2 cloves garlic, minced
1 cup celery, chopped
3 tablespoons butter
1/4 cup chili sauce
1 (8 ounce) can tomato sauce
1 (10 ounce) frozen package cut okra
1/2 cup long grain rice
1/4 teaspoon black pepper
1/4 teaspoon cayenne pepper

Combine ham bone, water, celery, carrot and onion. Bring to a boil. Simmer 45 minutes. Strain broth and discard vegetables and bone.

Sauté onion, garlic and celery in butter. Add broth. Add ham, tomato, chili sauce and rice. Bring to a boil. Simmer covered until rice is done.

Add okra and shrimp and cover. Heat five minutes. Season.

Serves six.

LEMON SHRIMP SOUP

1 pound raw shrimp, shelled and deveined
8 cups water
6 chicken bouillon cubes
3 small dried hot dried chilies
1 1/2 tablespoons crushed dry lemon grass
1/3 cup lemon juice
3 green onions, cut into 2 inch lengths
1/4 cup fresh cilantro, chopped

Combine water, bouillon cubes and chilies in large pan. Wrap lemon grass in cheese cloth and add to pan. Bring to a boil. Reduce heat. Cover and simmer for 20 minutes. Add shrimp. Cover and simmer until shrimp turn pink. Stir in onions and cilantro. Remove lemon grass and serve.

Serves six.

MIDNIGHT SUN SOUP

1 1/2 pounds raw shrimp, shelled and deveined
1/4 cup vegetable oil
2 tablespoons flour
1 large onion, chopped
1 large green pepper, chopped
12 ears fresh corn, cut kernels from cob
1/2 cup tomato sauce
water
salt to taste
pepper to taste

Make a roux of flour and oil by heating and cooking until it is brown and thick. Add onion and sauté. Add green pepper, corn and tomato sauce. Add enough water to desired consistency. Simmer about 30 minutes.

Add shrimp and simmer about 15 minutes. Season with salt and pepper.

Serves eight.

PEA SOUP WITH SHRIMP

2 (4 1/2 ounce) cans shrimp, drained
3 cubes beef bouillon
3 cups hot water
1/2 cup onion, chopped
1 large carrot, cubed
1/2 teaspoon dry sage
1/2 teaspoon tarragon
1 (10 ounce) package frozen peas
1/2 cup light cream
1/2 cup dry sherry
salt to taste
pepper to taste

Combine bouillon, water, onion and carrot. Boil until vegetables are tender. Add herbs and peas. Bring to a boil. Blend mixture until pureed. Return to pan. Add shrimp, cream and sherry. Season. Heat and serve.

Serves four.

PRINCE WILLIAM SOUND GUMBO

1 pound raw shrimp, shelled and deveined
2 medium onions, sliced
1 green pepper, chopped
2 cloves garlic, minced
1/2 cup butter
2 tablespoons flour
1 (8 ounce) can tomato sauce
1 (10 ounce) package frozen okra
1 (15 ounce) can tomatoes, chopped with liquid reserved
2 beef bouillon cubes
1 1/2 cups hot water
2 tablespoons Worcestershire sauce
1/8 teaspoon powdered cloves
1/2 teaspoon dried basil, crumbled
2 bay leaves
1/4 teaspoon fresh ground pepper

Sauté onions, garlic and pepper in butter. Blend in flour. Stir until smooth. Dissolve bouillon cubes in hot water and add to vegetables. Stir until smooth. Add remaining ingredients, except shrimp. Simmer and stir occasionally about 35 minutes. Serve over hot rice.

Serves six.

SEAFOOD GUMBO

2 pounds raw shrimp, shelled and deveined
1 pound crab meat, flaked
1 cup ham, chopped
1 pint oysters
1/4 cup vegetable oil
3 pounds fresh okra, sliced thin
1/3 cup vegetable oil
1/3 cup flour
1 quart water
2 tablespoons tomato paste
1/2 cup fresh parsley, chopped
2 cloves garlic, minced
3 bay leaves
1 cup celery, chopped
hot pepper sauce to taste
cooked rice

Sauté okra in 1/4 cup oil until soft and thickened. Set aside.

In a heavy pot, cook and stir paste made of oil and flour, until thick and brown. Add onion, water and tomato paste. Stir in okra, shrimp, crab, ham and oysters. Stir in parsley, garlic, bay leaves and celery. Simmer uncovered for one hour. Season to taste and serve over rice.

Serves twelve.

SEWARD SHRIMP BISQUE

1 1/3 cups cooked shrimp, shelled and deveined
1/2 cup tomato paste
2 1/2 cups chicken stock
1/2 red onion, finely chopped
1/3 cup light cream
1/4 teaspoon paprika
1 tablespoon parsley, chopped
1 tablespoon chives, chopped
6 cooked shrimp for garnish
salt to taste
pepper to taste

Combine shrimp, chicken stock, tomato paste and onion. Blend into a smooth puree. Pour puree into a pan and heat until just below the boiling point. Add cream and paprika. Season to taste. Cook over low heat for two minutes. Garnish with shrimp, parsley and chives.

Serves six.

SHRIMP AND CORN CHOWDER

1 (4 1/2 ounce) can shrimp
1 can cream style corn
2 cups chicken broth
1 teaspoon fresh dill, snipped
1 teaspoon parsley, chopped
salt to taste
pepper to taste

Combine corn and chicken broth. Simmer for five minutes. Add salt and pepper to taste. Add shrimp, dill and parsley. Simmer three minutes. Do not boil.

Serves four.

SHRIMP CIOPPINO

2/3 pound raw shrimp, shelled and deveined
2 2/3 pounds raw lobster tails,
    shelled and cut into serving pieces
1 1/2 pounds halibut, cut up
2 (10 1/2 ounce) cans clams
1/2 medium onion, minced
3 cloves garlic, minced
1 tablespoon fresh parsley, snipped
1/4 cup olive oil
3 1/2 cups tomato
2 (8 ounce) cans seasoned tomato sauce
1 1/2 cups water
dash pepper
1 teaspoon salt
1/2 teaspoon crushed oregano
1/2 teaspoon marjoram
1/2 cup cooking sherry

    Sauté onion, garlic and parsley in oil. Add tomatoes, tomato sauce, water and seasonings. Cover. Bring to a boil. Reduce heat. Simmer uncovered 30 minutes. Add sherry the last ten minutes.

    Add fish and seafood to hot sauce. Cover and bring to boil. Cook over low heat for 15 minutes.

    Serves six.

SHRIMP GAZPACHO

1 (4 1/2 ounce) can shrimp, reserve liquid
1 cucumber, unpeeled and sliced
1 medium onion, sliced
1 green pepper, seeded and sliced
1 clove garlic
1/4 cup fresh parsley
4 cups tomato juice
1/4 teaspoon hot pepper sauce
2 tablespoons olive oil
juice of one lemon
pepper to taste

Chill shrimp, vegetables and tomato juice. In blender, place cucumber, onion, green pepper, garlic and parsley. Process to almost pureed. Combine with tomato juice, pepper sauce, olive oil, lemon juice, shrimp and liquid. Serve well chilled. Season.
Serves four.

SHRIMP SOUP

2 pounds raw shrimp, shelled and deveined
2 quarts of water
3 large yellow onions, peeled and chopped
2 garlic cloves, minced
1/4 cup olive oil
4 large ripe tomatoes, peeled, cored,
  seeded and coarsely chopped
3 tablespoons parsley, minced
2 large bay leaves
1/4 cup tomato paste
1/2 teaspoon pepper, freshly ground
1/2 teaspoon cayenne pepper
1 cup dry white wine
1 teaspoon salt
1/4 cup fresh coriander, chopped

Place shrimp and water in large pan. Bring to a simmer. Drain at once. Reserve shrimp and cooking water.

In a separate pan sauté onions and garlic in olive oil five to six minutes. Add tomatoes, parsley, bay leaves, tomato paste, black and cayenne peppers. Cover and simmer 25 minutes. Add shrimp cooking water and wine. Simmer uncovered for one hour.

Add shrimp and salt heat for five minutes. Discard bay leaves. Sprinkle with coriander and serve.

Serves six.

SUMMER SHRIMP CREAM SOUP

1 (4 1/2 ounce) can shrimp
1 medium head iceberg lettuce, trimmed and cored
1 onion, sliced
2 cups water
1 tablespoon butter
2 cubes chicken bouillon
1/4 cup heavy cream
salt to taste
pepper to taste
dash nutmeg

Cut lettuce in fourths. Place in large pan with onions and water. Cover and cook over medium heat five minutes. Strain and reserve liquid. Add butter and bouillon cubes to liquid and set aside.

Puree lettuce an onion in a blender. Add puree, cream, shrimp to seasoned liquid. Season. Heat and serve with a dash of nutmeg. This soup can be chilled and served cold.

Servers five.

VALDEZ SHRIMP BISQUE

1/2 pound cooked shrimp, shelled and deveined
2/3 cup clam juice
2 cups heavy cream
1/4 teaspoon paprika
1/2 cup dry sherry
1 tablespoon fresh parsley, finely chopped
1 tablespoon fresh chives, finely chopped
salt to taste
pepper to taste

Blend shrimp and clam juice for one minute. Remove and place in the top of a double boiler. Add cream and paprika, salt and pepper. Cook over hot water, stirring until soup boils. Add sherry and serve immediately.

Garnish with chives and parsley.

Serves four.

VEGETABLE SHRIMP CHOWDER

2 1/2 pounds raw shrimp, shelled and deveined
6 cups water, boiling
1 small onion, chopped
3 bay leaves
1 tablespoon vinegar
4 slices bacon, chopped and fried crisp
1 green pepper, chopped
2 stalks celery, chopped
2 small onions, chopped
2 potatoes, diced
1 (16 ounce) can tomatoes, chopped

Add shrimp, one small onion, bay leaves and vinegar to boiling water. Cook five minutes. Remove shrimp and set aside. Strain water and save.

Fry bacon. Add green peppers, celery and onions until soft. Add potatoes and tomatoes. Simmer 20 minutes. Add shrimp liquid and boil. Add shrimp and cook to heat the shrimp.

Serves six.

BAKED SHRIMP SANDWICHES

1 (4 1/2 ounce) can shrimp, drained
8 slices whole wheat bread, buttered
1 cup Swiss cheese, grated
3 eggs, lightly beaten
1 1/2 cups chicken bouillon
2 teaspoons Worcestershire sauce
1 tablespoon Dijon style mustard
dash nutmeg

Place four slices of bread in an eight inch baking dish with buttered side down. Sprinkle half of the cheese on the bread. Top cheese with shrimp. Top shrimp with remaining cheese. Cover with remaining bread slices buttered side up. Whisk eggs, broth, Worcestershire sauce and nutmeg. Pour over bread. Bake about 40 minutes at 350 degree.

Serves four.

CREAMED SHRIMP ON TOAST

1 pound cooked shrimp, shelled and deveined
2 tablespoons butter
3 green onion, chopped
2 tablespoons flour
1 cup sour cream
1/4 cup water
salt to taste
pepper to taste
toast

Coat shrimp and onions with flour. Sauté shrimp and onions in butter five minutes. Add 1/4 cup water and stir in cream. Simmer until thickened and heated through. Season to taste. Serve on buttered toast.
Serves four.

CREAMED SHRIMP WITH WINE ON TOAST

1 pound raw shrimp, shelled and deveined
1/4 cup onions, finely chopped
1/4 cup butter
1 cup dry white wine
1 cup whipping cream
1/4 teaspoon salt
pepper to taste
flour
toast

Coat shrimp with flour. Sauté shrimp and onions in butter for two to three minutes. Remove mixture from pan. Add wine, cream, salt and pepper. Cook stirring constantly until thickened and smooth. Return shrimp to pan and heat thoroughly. Serve on toast.

Serves four.

SANDWICHES

EGG AND SHRIMP SALAD SANDWICH

1 cup cooked shrimp
3 hard boiled eggs, chopped
1/2 cup walnuts, chopped
1/2 cup mayonnaise
2 cups alfalfa sprouts
4 pita breads

Combine eggs, nuts and shrimp. Fold in mayonnaise. Fill pita with shrimp mixture and sprouts.
Serves four.

HOT SHRIMP BURGERS

1/2 pound raw shrimp, shelled and deveined
1/2 pound hot bulk pork sausage
1/2 cup green onions, chopped
1 clove garlic, minced
2 tablespoon salad oil
hamburger buns

Grind shrimp in a food processor. Add sausage, onions and garlic. Process until mixture is smooth. Shape into patties. Fry until golden. Serve on hamburger buns.
Serves six.

SHRIMP BAGELS

1 (4 1/2 ounce) can shrimp, drained
1 cup mozzarella cheese, shredded
1/4 cup green onion, chopped
1/4 teaspoon garlic powder
1 tablespoon butter
2 tablespoon fresh parsley, chopped
1 tablespoon fresh basil, chopped
2 bagels, split

Sprinkle cheese over four bagel halves. Broil until cheese is melted and bubbly. Sauté shrimp with green onion, garlic powder, parsley and basil in butter. Divide mixture between the bagel halves.

Serves four.

SHRIMP CHEESE SANDWICH

**1/2 pound cooked shrimp, shelled, deveined
    and coarsely chopped
1 cup cheddar cheese, grated
2 tablespoons butter
1/8 cup onion, minced
1 tablespoon lemon juice
2 tablespoons Worcestershire sauce
1/4 teaspoon paprika
black ground pepper to taste
6 rolls, split and lightly buttered**

Combine first seven ingredients. Fold in shrimp. Fill rolls with shrimp mixture. Broil until bubbly and lightly browned.
    Serves six.

SHRIMP SALAD IN CROISSANTS

1 cup cooked shrimp, shelled and deveined
2 cups leaf lettuce, shredded
1 medium carrot, shredded
4 large radishes, shredded
1 cup alfalfa sprouts
2 green onions, sliced
1/4 cup walnuts, chopped
creamy cucumber dressing
4 croissants, split lengthwise

Combine the first seven ingredients and spoon onto bottom halves of the croissant. Top each with some dressing and cover with the croissant top.

Serves four.

TOASTO SHRIMP

1/2 pound raw shrimp, shelled and deveined
1 tablespoon peanut oil
2 1/2 teaspoons curry powder
1 medium onion, chopped
1 small red bell pepper, chopped
1/4 cup mango chutney
1 small tomato, seeded and chopped
1/4 cup mayonnaise
1 French bread baguette, sliced
1 teaspoon soy sauce
salt to taste
pepper to taste

    Sauté shrimp with oil and curry until shrimp are just pink. Transfer shrimp to a bowl and cool. Sauté onion, pepper and curry about ten minutes. Add chutney and soy sauce. Cook for one minute. Set aside. Chop shrimp and return to bowl. Add vegetables and tomato. Add mayonnaise to shrimp mixture. Season with salt and pepper.
    Toast bread. Cool slightly and top with shrimp mixture.
    Serves six.

ISLAND SHRIMP KABOBS

1 1/2 pounds raw shrimp, shelled and deveined
4 slices bacon
1 (28 ounce) can sliced pineapple
1 tablespoon Dijon style mustard
juice of one lime
1 teaspoon sugar
1 teaspoon salt
8 tablespoons butter
pepper to taste
dash of cayenne pepper

Cut bacon in squares and pineapples slices in quarters. Alternate pieces of each with shrimp on skewers. Combine remaining ingredients and brush sauce over kabobs. Grill 6-8 inches over medium hot coals. Turn skewers as needed. Baste frequently.

Serves three.

ITALIAN SHRIMP RICE

12 ounces raw shrimp, shelled and deveined
2 tablespoons olive oil
2 tablespoons red onion, diced
1 1/4 cups long grain white rice
1/3 cup dry white wine
5 cups unsalted chicken broth
1 cup peas
1 teaspoon lemon rind, grated
1 tablespoon fresh lemon juice
salt to taste
pepper to taste
fresh parsley for garnish

Sauté onion in olive oil. Stir in rice and coat with oil. Add wine and heat to boiling. Stir over high heat until wine is almost evaporated. Stir in 1 cup broth and stir until broth is absorbed. Continue adding 1/2 cup at a time stirring constantly. With the last cup of broth add shrimp, peas and lemon. Cook uncovered until broth is absorbed. Season and garnish.

Serves four.

MEDITERRANEAN SHRIMP LOAF

2 cups cooked shrimp, shelled, deveined and chopped
1 pound French bread
1 tomato, finely diced
4 green onions, finely diced
1/2 cup black olives
1/2 cup stuffed green olives
6 cloves garlic, minced
2 tablespoons parsley, chopped
pinch thyme
2 tablespoons capers
2 tablespoons olive oil
1/2 cup fresh parmesan, grated
salt to taste
pepper to taste
juice of one lemon
Tabasco to taste

Cut loaf of bread in half and scoop out inside of both halves. Grind bread from insides to medium fine crumbs. Combine tomato, onions, olives, garlic, parsley, thyme capers, salt, pepper, lemon olive oil and tobacco. Mix well. Add shrimp and cheese to bread mixture. Mix well. Brush oil on hollowed out bread. Pack mixture into hollow of bread. Place halves of bread together and wrap tightly with foil. Refrigerate overnight. Cut into 1/2 inch slices. Garnish with olives and parsley.
Serves twelve.

MINI SHRIMP CREPES

1 cup cooked shrimp, chopped
1/4 cup mayonnaise
1/8 teaspoon salt
4 eggs
4 egg yolks
2 1/4 cups milk
1/4 cup brandy
2 cups flour
1 teaspoon salt
1/4 cup butter, melted

Mix shrimp, mayonnaise and salt. Set aside.

Beat eggs, egg yolks, milk and brandy. Add flour and salt. Beat until smooth. Stir in butter and let batter stand 30 minutes at room temperature. Lightly grease a heated skillet. Stir batter and pour about one tablespoon into center of pan; immediately tilt pan to spread batter over the bottom. Cook about 30 seconds just until bottom is lightly browned. Turn and cook other side. Stack crepes on a flat surface and cover. Fill crepes and roll up to server.

Serves four.

PRINCE WILLIAM SOUND STIR FRIED SHRIMP

1 pound raw shrimp, shelled and deveined
3/4 cup chicken broth
1 tablespoon cornstarch
2 tablespoons dry sherry
1 tablespoon soy sauce
1 tablespoon rice vinegar
1/2 teaspoon sugar
1/4 teaspoon hot red pepper, crushed
2 bunches spinach, cleaned and tear into small pieces
3 tablespoons oil
3 cloves garlic, minced
1 tablespoon fresh ginger root, minced
salt to taste

Combine chicken broth and cornstarch, with sherry, soy sauce, vinegar, sugar and hot pepper. Set aside. When wok is very hot add one tablespoon oil and spinach. Stir to coat spinach thoroughly. Stir fry until leaves are wilted and turn green. Season to taste with salt. Transfer to plate and keep warm. Reheat wok and add two tablespoons oil, garlic, ginger root and shrimp. Stir fry about three minutes. Stir sauce mixture and then stir in shrimp. Cook and stir until thick. Pour shrimp and sauce over spinach.
Serves four.

SKEWERED SHRIMP WITH CURRY APRICOT GLAZE

1 1/2 pounds raw shrimp, shelled and deveined
3 tablespoons olive oil
3 tablespoons apricot preserves
1 1/2 tablespoons white wine vinegar
2 1/4 teaspoons Dijon style mustard
2 1/4 teaspoons curry powder
1 1/4 teaspoons garlic, minced
12 10 inch bamboo skewers
shredded iceberg lettuce
lemon wedges for garnish

Whisk the first seven ingredients except shrimp in a large bowl. Add shrimp and toss to coat. Cover and refrigerate for two hours. Soak skewers in water for about 30 minutes. Place shrimp on skewers. Broil shrimp about six inched from heat for about three minutes per side. Place shredded lettuce on platter and arrange skewers on top. Garnish with lemon.
Serves six.

SHRIMP AND BEEF STIR FRY

1/2 pound raw shrimp, shelled and deveined
1/2 pound beef, sliced thin
2 tablespoons cornstarch
2 teaspoons soy sauce
3 tablespoons soy sauce
2 teaspoons dry sherry
1 tablespoon dry sherry
1/2 teaspoon fresh ginger root, minced
1 clove garlic, minced
1 pound fresh broccoli, cut into bite size pieces
3 tablespoons vegetable oil
2 carrots, cut diagonally into thin slices
1 onions, chunked
1/2 cup water

Coat beef with a mixture of one tablespoon cornstarch, two teaspoons soy sauce and sherry, ginger and garlic. Let stand 15 minutes. Blend remaining cornstarch, soy sauce, sherry and 1/2 cup water and set aside. Heat wok and add one teaspoon oil and shrimp. Stir fry 30 seconds. Add beef and stir fry one minute. Remove. Heat remaining oil in wok and stir fry broccoli, carrots and onion for two minutes. Sprinkle two tablespoon water over vegetables and steam covered for three minutes. Add shrimp and beef mixture to sauce and cook until sauce boils and thickens in about one minute.

Serves four.

SHRIMP AND GRITS

2 pounds raw shrimp, shelled and deveined
6 cups water
1/2 teaspoon salt
2 cups quick cooking grits
1 cup sharp cheddar cheese, grated
pinch of nutmeg
hot pepper sauce
12 slices of bacon
1/2 pound mushrooms, sliced
2 cups green onions, sliced
2 large cloves garlic, minced
2 1/2 tablespoons lemon juice
fresh parsley for garnish

Boil water and salt in a large pan. Whisk in grits. Reduce heat. Cover and simmer until mixture is thick and grits are tender. Whisk in cheese and nutmeg. Season to taste with pepper sauce. Cover and set aside.

Brown bacon in skillet. Remove bacon and discard half of the drippings. Add shrimp to skillet and cook until pink. Remove shrimp. Add mushroom and sauté. Add green onions and garlic and sauté. Return shrimp and bacon to skillet. Mix in lemon juice. Season with salt, pepper and hot sauce. Spoon grits onto plates. Spoon shrimp over grits and season.

Serves four.

SHRIMP AND PASTA

12 ounces raw shrimp, shelled and deveined
3 tablespoons olive oil
3 large garlic cloves, chopped
1/2 teaspoon dried red pepper, crushed
1 (28-ounce) can Italian plum tomatoes,
    chopped with juices reserved
1 10-ounce can baby clams, drained with juices reserved
4 tablespoons fresh parsley, chopped
1 teaspoon dried basil, crumbed
1 teaspoon anchovy paste
1 teaspoon anchovy paste
salt to taste
pepper to tastse
12 ounces large shell pasta, cooked

Heat oil over medium head. Add garlic and pepper and sauté for one minute. Mix in tomatoes and clams with juices, two tablespoons parsley, basil and anchovy paste. Cover skillet and cook 15 minutes. Uncover and simmer until sauce thickens, stirring occasionally. Add clams and shrimp. Simmer until shrimp are just cooked thorough, about three minutes. Season with salt and pepper.

Add pasta to sauce and toss. Garnish with parsley.
Serves four.

SHRIMP KABOBS

1 1/2 pounds raw shrimp, shelled and deveined
4 slices bacon
1 (28 ounce) can sliced pineapple
1 tablespoon Dijon style mustard
juice of one lime
1 teaspoon sugar
1 teaspoon salt
8 tablespoons butter
pepper to taste
dash of cayenne pepper

Cut bacon in squares and pineapples slices in quarters. Spear alternating pieces of each on skewers. Combine remaining ingredients and brush sauce over kabobs. Grill 6-8 inches over medium hot coals. Turn the skewers as needed and baste frequently.
Serves three.

SHRIMP PAELLA

1/2 pound raw shrimp, shelled and deveined
1/2 pound clams
1/2 pound mussels
1/2 pound salmon, cut into 1/2 inch squares
2 tablespoons olive oil
1 large onion, chopped
1 green onion, chopped
1 green pepper, chopped
2 mild green chilies, diced
1/8 cup celery, chopped
3 cloves garlic, chopped
1/4 pound dry Chorizo sausage
2 cups Roma tomatoes, chopped
1/2 cup tomato sauce
1/8 cup white wine
juice of 1/2 lemon
1 cup uncooked white rice
1 tablespoon fresh cilantro, chopped
1 tablespoon fresh parsley, chopped
1 tablespoon chili powder
pinch saffron threads
2 tablespoons green olives, sliced
1/2 cup frozen peas

Sauté onion, pepper and chilies, celery and garlic in olive oil. Add tomatoes, tomato sauce, sausage, wine and lemon juice. Simmer 15 minutes. Add cilantro, parsley, chili powder and saffron. Simmer 5 minutes. Add one cup rice and stir. Cover and simmer 5 minutes. Stir again until rice is almost tender. Add clams, mussels, shrimp, salmon and peas. Cover and simmer 7 minutes. Remove from heat and serve.

Serves five.

SHRIMP PASTA PRIMAVERA

2 pounds cooked shrimp, shelled and deveined
1 pound spinach noodles, cooked
2 tablespoons olive oil
2 tablespoons sunflower oil
1 garlic clove, crushed
1 slice ginger, peeled
1/4 cup sesame seeds
1/4 pound snow peas
1 zucchini, sliced
1 green pepper, sliced
1 red pepper, sliced
1 bound broccoli floret
1 carrot, sliced diagonally
1 pound summer squash, cut into strips
1/4 pound cabbage, cut into chunks
pepper to taste
salt to taste

Sauté olive and sunflower oils, garlic and ginger. Discard ginger and garlic. Stir in sesame seeds and toast lightly. Add remaining vegetables. Stir fry over high heat until tender. Toss lightly with pasta and shrimp. Serve at room temperature or chilled.

Serves ten.

SHRIMP SCAMPI

1 pound raw shrimp, shelled, deveined and
**   butterflied leaving tails attached**
1 cup butter, melted
1/4 cup olive oil
1 tablespoon parsley, chopped
3/4 teaspoon dried basil
1/2 teaspoon dried oregano
1 clove garlic, minced
3/4 teaspoon salt
1 tablespoon lemon juice

Mix all ingredients except shrimp. Place shrimp in a shallow pan tails up. Pour sauce and bake for five minutes at 250 degrees. Broil for five minutes to brown.
Serves six.

SITKA STIR FRIED SHRIMP

1 pound raw shrimp, shelled and deveined
6 green shallots, trimmed and chopped
1 tablespoon peanut oil
1 clove garlic, crushed
small piece green ginger, peeled and grated
1 chili, shredded
1 tablespoon soy sauce
1 tablespoon vinegar
fresh coriander sprigs, chopped
pinch of Chinese five spice
toasted sesame seeds
3 cups rice, cooked and hot

Heat oil in wok and quickly stir fry shrimp and shallots. Add garlic, ginger, chili, soy sauce, vinegar, five spice and coriander. Serve with hot rice sprinkled with toasted sesame seeds.

Serves four.

SPICY CAJUN GRILLED SHRIMP

32 large raw shrimp, shelled and deveined
1/2 cup soy sauce
1/2 cup olive oil
5 tablespoons Cajun seasoning mix
1/4 cup oriental sesame oil
1/4 cup fresh lemon juice
2 tablespoons fresh ginger, minced
2 teaspoons dry mustard
2 teaspoons hot pepper sauce

Mix ingredients and marinate in large bowl. Add shrimp and let stand for 20 minutes.

Remove shrimp from marinade and grill until pink and cooked, about two minutes per side.

Serves eight.

SPICY SEAFOOD KABOBS

12 large raw shrimp, shelled and deveined
1 pound smoked salmon, cubed
1 red pepper, cubed
1 green pepper, cubed
2 large peaches, cubed
2 tablespoons peanut oil
1/8 cup orange juice
juice of one lime
juice of one lemon
1 tablespoon rice wine vinegar
2 tablespoons white wine
3 garlic cloves, mashed
1 tablespoon fresh ginger, grated
1 tablespoons fresh hot chilies, chopped
1 clove
2 tablespoons honey
1 tablespoon tomato paste
1 tablespoon fresh cilantro, chopped
1 tablespoon dry mustard
salt to taste

Alternate salmon, shrimp, pepper and peaches on skewers. Combine remaining ingredients. Bring to boil, then simmer until reduced by 1/3. Baste skewers and grill until done about three minutes per side.

Serves four.

STIR FRIED SHRIMP

1 pound raw shrimp, shelled and deveined
3/4 cup chicken broth
1 tablespoon cornstarch
2 tablespoons dry sherry
1 tablespoon soy sauce
1 tablespoon rice vinegar
1/2 teaspoon sugar
1/4 teaspoon hot red pepper, crushed
2 bunches spinach, cleaned and torn into small pieces
3 tablespoons oil
3 cloves garlic, minced
1 tablespoon fresh ginger root, minced
salt to taste

Combine chicken broth, cornstarch, sherry, soy sauce, vinegar, sugar and hot pepper. Set aside.

When wok is very hot add one tablespoon oil and spinach. Stir to coat spinach thoroughly. Stir fry until leaves are wilted and turn green. Season to taste with salt. Transfer to plate and keep warm.

Reheat wok and add two tablespoons oil, garlic, ginger root and shrimp. Stir fry about three minutes. Stir in chicken broth mixture. Add shrimp. Cook and stir until thick. Pour shrimp and sauce over spinach.

Serves four.

THAI SHRIMP NOODLES

1/2 pound cooked cocktail shrimp, shelled and deveined
1/2 pound linguine, cooked
3/4 cup tomato juice, no added salt variety
3 tablespoon soy sauce
1 tablespoon vinegar
2 teaspoons sugar
3/4 teaspoon cornstarch
3 tablespoons vegetable oil, divided
1/2 pound chicken breast, cut into strips
2 cloves garlic, minced
1/2 pound fresh bean sprouts, rinsed and drained
1/3 cup green onions, sliced
1 tablespoon cilantro, minced
lime wedges

Combine tomato juice, soy sauce, vinegar, sugar and cornstarch. Heat one tablespoon oil in a hot wok. Add chicken and stir fry one minute. Stir in linguine and cook until heated through. Add chicken, shrimp, cilantro and tomato juice mixture. Cook until sauce boils and thickens, stir to keep from sticking. Serve with lime wedges.

Serves four.

REMOVING CRAB MEAT

Remove crab meat using this technique. All that's needed is a mallet, wood block, container to catch meat and some shaking.

CRAB BODY
Break body cartilage by squeezing the body cavity with the palm of your hand. Rap body over container. Most of the meat will fall out. Tear away cartilage and shake out meat.

LEG MEAT
Separate leg from the body. Start with smallest leg section and work to the largest. Pull smallest leg section off first. Lay the next leg section bottom side down on the wood block and strike with mallet to crack shell but not crush it. Strike leg over container. Pull empty section off.

Repeat process for all leg sections.

CRAB CLAW
Pull moveable pincher up and out. Lay claw on wood block and strike it. Remove broken pieces of shell and shake meat out. Lay knuckle on the wood block and strike it. Remove shell fragments and shake meat out.

Pull empty knuckle off and repeat process for end section.

PREPARING CRAB

Crabs can be cooked whole (live) or cleaned with back and viscera removed. There is a taste difference. It is important to cook crabs live or immediately after they are killed. Here are several ways to cook and remove crab meat.

WHOLE LIVE CRAB

whole live crabs
1 pint water, boiling
1/2 cup cider vinegar
1 teaspoon cayenne pepper

Drop live crabs in a large pot containing seasoned boiling water. Cover and steam for ten minutes until shell are pink. Remove and cool. Break off claws and legs at body, crack and removed meat. Pull top shell off from body. Scrape off white colored gill from sides. Remove spongy digestive parts located in the middle of body. Slice or break top of the inner skeleton at the front. Remove meat from back and pockets.

WHOLE CLEANED CRAB

whole live crabs
1 pint water, boiling
1 teaspoon cayenne

Kill crab instantly by grasping the legs firmly and bring crab swiftly down abdomen first over a solid edge. This will split the crab. Discard back, mouth, gills and abdomen flap. Wash to remove the viscera. Steam crab in boiling seasoned water for ten minutes until they turn pink. Break or cut off claws and legs at the body. Crack and remove meat.

ALMOND CRAB SPREAD

1/2 pound crab meat
8 ounces cream cheese
2 tablespoons milk
1 tablespoon horseradish
1 teaspoon Worcestershire sauce
dash Tabasco sauce
1 teaspoon lemon juice
1/3 cup almonds, sliced

Beat cheese with milk until soft. Add crab, chives, horseradish, Worcestershire, Tabasco and lemon juice. Blend well.

Spoon mixture into a serving dish. Sprinkle almonds over the top. Bake for 25 minutes at 375 degrees.

Serves four.

COTTAGE CHEESE CRAB DIP

1/3 cup crab meat, flaked
1 cup cottage cheese
2 tablespoons milk
2 sprigs fresh dill, minced

Blend ingredients thoroughly. Serve with crackers or vegetables.

Serves four.

CRAB AND AVOCADO SUSHI ROLLS

1/2 pound crab meat, flaked
1/2 medium avocado, peeled and mashed
1/2 teaspoon wasabi powder
2 teaspoons mayonnaise
salt to taste
lemon juice
2 cups seasoned sushi rice, cooked
2 sheets nori seaweed

Mix avocado with wasabi powder and mayonnaise. Season to taste with salt and lemon juice. Sprinkle crab meat with lemon juice.

Roll rice into two even rolls the length of the seaweed. Place a sheet of the seaweed on a work surface. Arrange a roll of rice at on end. Spread half the avocado mixture along length of rice and then arrange half the crab meat along the seaweed. Roll up carefully. Chill until required. Cut each roll into six pieces.

Serves two.

CRAB AND CUCUMBER ROLLS

1 1/2 cups crab meat, shredded
3 cucumbers, peeled
salt to taste
2/3 cup yogurt
3 tablespoons lemon juice

Slice cucumbers lengthwise into one inch strips. Remove seeds and soft center.

Place a small mound of crab at one end of the cucumber strip and roll up. Secure with a wood toothpick. Arrange crab rolls on serving dish and chill.

Blend yogurt and lemon juice. Serve dipping sauce with crab rolls.

Serves two.

CRAB AVOCADO

8 ounces crab meat
1/3 cup celery, chopped
3 hard cooked eggs, chopped
2 tablespoons pimiento, chopped
1 tablespoon onion, chopped
1/2 teaspoon salt
1/2 cup mayonnaise
3 avocados
lemon juice
salt to taste
3 tablespoons bread crumbs
1 teaspoon butter, melted
2 tablespoons almond, slivered

Mix crab, celery, eggs pimiento, onion, salt and mayonnaise.

Cut avocados in half lengthwise. Brush cut surfaces with lemon juice. Sprinkle with salt. Fill avocado halves with crab mixture. Toss crumbs with butter and spread over crab mixture.

Place avocados in shallow baking dish. Bake at 400 degrees uncovered for ten minutes. Sprinkle almonds over crumb topping. Bake five minutes until bubbly.

Serves six.

CRAB CANAPÉS

1 cup crab meat
1 teaspoon butter
2 shallots, minced
1/4 green pepper, chopped
3/4 cup fresh mushrooms, chopped
2 tablespoons pimento, diced
1/4 teaspoon mustard
2 tablespoons white wine
1/4 cup cream
2 egg yolks, beaten lightly
dash of cayenne
salt to taste
pepper to taste
8 bread slices, toasted and cut in squares
8 slices cheese, cut in squares

Sauté shallots, pepper and mushrooms in butter. Add pimento, mustard and wine. Stir in cream and crab. remove from heat and stir in egg yolks. Season to taste. Spread on toast and top with cheese. Bake on cookie sheet at 350 degrees until cheese melts.

Serves eight.

CRAB CARDINAL

12 ounces crab meat, flaked
1 pound cooked shrimp, shelled and deveined
1 1/2 cup fresh mushrooms, sliced
1 1/2 cups butter
1/4 cup flour
1 1/4 cup milk
2 tablespoons dry sherry
1 tablespoon lemon juice
1/2 teaspoon lemon juice
1/2 teaspoon Worcestershire sauce
1/8 teaspoon slat
dash hot pepper sauce
1 cup soft bead crumbs
2 tablespoons butter, melted
1 cup Swiss cheese, shredded

Sauté mushrooms in 1/4 cup butter. Stir in flour until smooth. Add milk. Cook and stir until thickened and bubbly. Stir in crab, shrimp, sherry, lemon juice, Worcestershire sauce, salt and pepper sauce.

Spoon mixture into baking shells. Toss bread crumbs and butter. Sprinkle mixture over each baking dish. Bake at 350 degrees for 20 minutes. Sprinkle with cheese. Bake five minutes until cheese is melted.

Serves nine.

CRAB CHEESECAKE

1 cup crab meat
1 cup Ritz crackers
3 tablespoons butter, melted
2 (8 ounce) packages cream cheese, softened
3 eggs
1/4 cup sour cream
1 teaspoon fresh lemon juice
2 teaspoons onion, grated
1/2 teaspoon chowder seasoning
2 drops Tabasco sauce
1/2 teaspoon fresh ground pepper
1/2 cup sour cream

Mix butter and crackers. With the mixture line a nine inch springfrom pan. Bake at 350 degrees for ten minutes. Set aside to cool. Reduce oven to 325 degrees.

Beat cheese, eggs and 1/4 sour cream. Add lemon juice, onion, chowder seasoning, Tabasco and pepper. Stir in crab and mix well. Pour the mixture into the cooled crust and bake 50 minutes. Remove from oven. Run a knife around edge of cake to loosen from pan. Cool cake on wire rack remove the sides of the pan. Spread cake with sour cream.

Serves twelve.

CRAB CLAWS

24 large crab claw meat
2 cups flour
1 1/4 cup milk
1 1/2 teaspoon baking powder
1 teaspoon curry powder
1/2 teaspoon salt
2 cups fresh coconut, shredded
2 cups oil for deep frying

Add 1/2 cup flour to a separate bowl. Combine in another bowl remaining flour, milk, powder, curry and salt. In two separate pans, place reserved flour and coconut. Dredge claws in flour, dip in batter and roll in coconut. Deep fry until deep brown.

Serves six.

CRAB COCKTAIL

6 ounces crab meat, flaked
1/2 cup French dressing
chives to taste
fresh parsley to taste

Mix dressing with spices. Add to crab meat and mix lightly. Serve with crackers.

CRAB DIP

8 ounce crab meat, flaked
1 (10 3/4 ounce) can cream of mushroom soup
1 package unflavored gelatin
3 tablespoons cold water
3/4 cup mayonnaise
6 ounces cream cheese
3 stalks celery, chopped
1 small onion, grated
fresh parsley for garnish

Dissolve gelatin in water. Add soup and stir in mayonnaise. Add cheese and blend until creamy. Stir in crab and vegetables.

Place mixture in oiled mold and refrigerate until set. Remove from mold. Garnish with parsley.

Serves sixteen.

CRAB MOUSSE SPREAD

12 ounces crab meat, chopped
1 (10 3/4 ounce) can cream of mushroom soup
1 1/2 enveloped plain gelatin
3 tablespoons cold water
1 teaspoon Worcestershire sauce
1 jar pimento, drained and chopped
8 ounces cream cheese
1 cup celery, chopped fine
1 cup onion, chopped fine
6 drops Tobasco sauce

Dissolve gelatin in cold water. Warm undulate sour over low heat. Add gelatin, stirring until dissolved. Stir in remaining ingredients.

Pour in mold and chill several hours until firm. Remove from mold.

Serves eight.

CRAB PUFFS

8 ounces crab meat, flaked
1/2 cup butter
1 cup extra sharp cheese, grated
2 tablespoons parmesan cheese
1/4 cup mayonnaise
5 drops Tabasco sauce
1 package English muffins, split

Cream butter and cheeses. Mix in mayonnaise, Tabasco and crab meat

Spread mixture on each muffin half. Cut each muffin into eighths and spread out on a cookie sheet. Broil until brown and bubbly.

Serves three.

CRAB SPREAD

2 cups crab meat, chopped fine
4 ounces cream cheese
1/3 cup sour cream
1/2 teaspoon curry powder
1/4 teaspoon salt
1/2 teaspoon lemon juice
1 tablespoon chives, chopped
1 tablespoon capers

Mix cheese and cream. Blend in curry powder, salt, lemon juice, chives and capers. Add crab and mix.

Serves four.

CRAB STUFFED ARTICHOKE

1/2 cup crab meat
3 large artichokes
1 tablespoon lemon juice
1 teaspoon salt
2 tablespoons lime juice
3 ounces cream cheese
3 tablespoons mayonnaise
1 1/2 teaspoons onion, grated
1 clove garlic, minced

Wash artichokes. Discard outer leaves. Remove stems and cut about 1/2 inch from thorny tips of each leaf. Cook in 2 inched of boiling water containing lemon juice and salt. Cook covered for 30 minutes until base can be easily pierced by fork. Remove and drain upside down. Refrigerate.

Mix remaining ingredients. Carefully fill artichokes and serve chilled.

Serves two.

CRAB STUFFED CELERY STALKS

6 ounces crab meat, flaked
1 tablespoon lemon juice
3 tablespoons mayonnaise
6 ounces Roquefort cheese
2 ounces cream cheese

Mix ingredients. Fill celery stalks with mixture.

CRAB STUFFED CUCUMBERS

1 cup crab meat, chopped
2 small cucumbers
salt to taste
lemon juice
3 tablespoons mayonnaise
1 teaspoon Worcestershire sauce
1 teaspoon onion, grated
1 teaspoon fresh parsley, minced
hard boiled egg yolk, sieved for garnish

Slice cucumbers in half lengthwise. Scoop out and discard seeds. Sprinkle with salt and lemon juice. Chill.

Mix mayonnaise, Worcestershire sauce, onion and parsley. Add crab and toss. Spoon mixture on cucumbers. Serve with garnish sprinkled on top.

Serves two.

CRAB STUFFED MUSHROOMS

1 cup crab meat, flaked
12 medium mushrooms
3 tablespoons butter
1/4 cup cracker meal
2 tablespoons mayonnaise
1/4 teaspoon white pepper
1 tablespoon dry white vermouth
1 tablespoon grated parmesan cheese
salt to taste
1 cup milk
fresh parsley for garnish

Remove stems from mushroom caps and discard. Wipe caps with a damp sponge and set aside.

Melt butter and mix with crab, cracker meal, mayonnaise, pepper, vermouth, grated cheese and salt. Stuff each cap with mixture. Place caps in baking dish. Pour in milk to just below the stuffing.

Bake at 300 degrees approximately 45 minutes. Remove to serving dish. Garnish with parsley.

Serves six.

CRAB STUFFED SHRIMP

1/2 pound crab meat, flaked
1 1/2 pounds cooked shrimp, shelled and deveined
1 teaspoon sugar
4 peppercorns
1/2 teaspoon dried parsley
2 1/4 teaspoons salt
2 tablespoons celery, minced
1 tablespoon scallion, minced
fresh ground black pepper to taste
1 teaspoon lemon juice
1/4 cup mayonnaise

Split each shrimp down the back removing a wedge of meat to form a cavity for stuffing. Chop shrimp wedges.

Combine chopped shrimp with remaining ingredients. Pack into shrimp cavities. Chill.

Serves four.

CRAB STUFFED ZUCCHINI

12 ounces crab meat
3 medium zucchini
8 ounces feta cheese
1 teaspoon dried mint
1 clove garlic, minced
2 tablespoons olive oil
fresh ground pepper to taste

Poach zucchini in boiling water for three minutes. Remove and cool. Slice zucchini lengthwise and scoop out pulp. Let the shell drain.

Mix crab, feta, mint, garlic, oil and pepper. Spoon mixture into zucchini shells and slice into 1 1/2 wide chunks.

Serves six.

CRAB TEMPURA

2 pounds crab meat, flaked
2 tablespoons fine crackers crumbs
2 eggs
1 cup ice water
1 cup flour
1/4 teaspoon salt
2 cups oil for deep frying
1 cup commercial tempura dipping sauce

Mix crab, one egg and crumbs. Flour hands and shape into balls. Refrigerate crab balls one hour.

Make a batter by beating egg and ice water, then add flour and salt. Stir but leave batter lumpy.

Dip crab balls into batter. Deep fry until golden brown. Drain on paper towels.

Serves three.

CRAB VENETIAN

18 ounces crab meat, flaked
3 tablespoons lemon juice
fresh ground black pepper
2 tablespoons virgin olive oil

Sprinkle lemon juice on crab meat. Pepper to taste. Dribble on olive oil. Toss lightly.

Sever with crackers.

CRAB WITH ARTICHOKE

1/2 cup crab meat
3 large artichokes
1 tablespoon lemon juice
1 teaspoon salt
2 tablespoons lime juice
3 ounces cream cheese
3 tablespoons mayonnaise
1 1/2 teaspoons onion, grated
1 clove garlic, minced

Wash artichokes. Discard outer leaves. Remove stems and cut about 1/2 inch from thorny tips of each leaf. Cook in 2 inched of boiling water containing lemon juice and salt. Cook covered for 30 minutes until base can be easily pierced by fork. Remove and drain upside down. Refrigerate.

Mix remaining ingredients. Carefully fill artichokes and serve chilled.

Serves two.

DEEP FRIED CRAB PUFFS

2 cups crab meat, flaked
1/2 cup chicken broth
1/2 cup heavy cream
1/4 cup mushrooms, minced
2 1/2 tablespoons butter
3 tablespoons flour
1/2 teaspoon salt
1/8 teaspoon white pepper
1/2 teaspoon tarragon
2 tablespoons parsley, minced
2 cup oil for deep frying

Combine broth and cream. Heat to scalding and keep hot. Sauté mushrooms in butter, then add flour. Add broth and whisk until sauce thickens. Cook three minutes. Remove from heat and stir in salt, pepper, tarragon, parsley and crab. Spread mixture on a platter and cool. Cover and refrigerate for one hour.

Shape crab mixture into small balls. Deep fry until golden brown. Drain on paper towel.

Serves four.

APPETIZERS

CRAB

DEVILED CRAB

1/2 pound crab meat
2 tablespoons scallions, sliced thin
1/4 cup celery, diced
1 small green pepper, diced
1 small red pepper, diced
1 teaspoon dry mustard
1/2 teaspoon lemon juice
pinch cayenne pepper
salt to taste
pepper to taste
1/2 cup Ritz cracker crumbs
1/2 cup cream
2 tablespoons fresh parsley, chopped
2 tablespoons butter, melted

Combine scallions, celery, green and red peppers. Season with mustard, lemon juice, cayenne pepper, salt and pepper. Add 1/4 cup of cracker crumbs and crab. Pour in cream and stir until blended.

Spoon mixture into six baking dishes. Sprinkle with cracker crumbs and garnish. Drizzle with melted butter.

Bake at 350 degrees for 25 minutes until brown and bubbly. Serves six.

EASY CRAB DIP

7 ounces crab meat, flaked
1/2 cup sour cream
1 teaspoon lemon juice
1/2 teaspoon Tabasco sauce
1/4 teaspoon horseradish
1/4 teaspoon salt
paprika
fresh parsley, chopped for garnish

Mix all ingredients together. Garnish with paprika and parsley.

Serves four.

HOT BUTTERED CRAB CANAPÉS

1 pound crab meat, flaked
2 tablespoons butter
juice of 1/2 lemon
1 ounce cognac
salt to taste
cayenne to taste
toast, buttered and quartered
paprika for garnish

Sauté crab in butter and lemon juice. Add cognac and season to taste. Serve on hot toast and garnish with paprika.

Serves six.

HOT CRAB APPETIZER

1 1/2 cups crab meat, drained
8 ounces cream cheese
2 tablespoons onion, chopped fine
2 tablespoons milk
1/2 teaspoon cream style horseradish
1/4 teaspoon salt
dash of pepper
1/3 cup almonds, sliced and toasted

    Combine first seven ingredients. Mix until well blended. Spoon into nine inch pie plate. Sprinkle with almonds. Bake at 375 degrees for 15 minutes.
    Serve as a dip or spread.

HOT CRAB APPETIZERS

18 ounces crab meat, flaked
3 tablespoons butter
1 1/2 cups onion, minced
1 cup green pepper, chopped
2 cups tomatoes, chopped
1 1/2 teaspoon salt
3/4 cup potatoes, diced
1/4 teaspoon pepper
1/4 cup half and half cream
1 egg, beaten slightly
1/4 cup dry bread crumbs
10 fresh mushroom caps

Sauté onions and green pepper in butter. Add crab, tomatoes, potatoes, salt and pepper. Cook 20 minutes, stir occasionally. Stir half and half into mixture

Brush ten six ounce custard cup with egg. Spoon in crab mixture. Sprinkle with crumbs. Top with mushrooms and dot with butter. Place on cookie sheet and bake at 350 degrees until golden.

Serves ten.

HOT CURRIED CRAB DIP

2 (4 1/2 ounce) can crab meat, drained
1 medium green pepper, chopped
1 tablespoon butter
3 green onions, chopped
2 cans condensed cream of mushroom soup
2 eggs, beaten
3 tablespoons pimentos, chopped
2 tablespoon curry powder

Sauté peppers and onions in butter. Add soup and bring to boil. Add crab meat and allow to boil for two minutes. Remove from heat and stir in eggs, pimentos and curry powder.
Serve with crackers.

JOYCE'S CRAB DIP

7 ounces crab meat, flaked
3 packages cream cheese
1 medium onion, chopped
1/4 bottle Worcestershire sauce
1 bottle chili sauce
horseradish to taste

Mix cheese, onion and Worcestershire sauce. Spread into 9"x 9" dish.
Sprinkle crab over cheese mixture.
Combine chili sauce and horseradish. Spread over top of crab.
Serves four.

MINI CRAB ROLL UPS

8 ounces crab meat, flaked
1 package chive cream cheese, whipped
2 tablespoons parsley, chopped
1 tablespoon onion, minced
15 slices white bread
1 pound bacon

Mix crab, cheese, parsley and onion. Trim bread crusts from bread. Spread crab mixture on each slice of bread. Roll bread in jelly roll fashion and cut rolls in thirds. Cut bacon in half. Roll a piece of bacon around each bread roll. Secure with wood toothpick. Place rolls on a baking sheet. Bake at 350 degrees for 25 minutes. Turn once during baking.
Serves five.

PICKLED CRAB

1 pound crab meat
1/3 cup tarragon vinegar
1/4 cup cider vinegar
2/3 cup olive oil
dash of slat
fresh ground black pepper to taste

Combine all ingredients except crab meat in a small bowl. Whisk vigorously. Refrigerate covered for two days.
Place crab meat in a shallow dish. Spoon dressing over it and serve immediately.
Serves eight.

POTTED CRAB

3 cups crab meat
1/2 cup butter, softened
lemon juice to taste
cayenne pepper to taste
anchovy paste to taste
fresh parsley, chopped for garnish

Pound crab in mortar with butter. Mix with lemon juice, anchovy paste and cayenne pepper. Pass smooth mixture through sieve and pack mixture into little pots. Pour melted butter over top of each pot and bake at 375 degrees for 20 minutes. Cool. Garnish with parsley.

Serves six.

SPICY CRAB DIP

6 ounces crab meat, flaked
2 packages cream cheese
1/2 cup sour cream
1/4 cup mayonnaise
2 tablespoons white wine
2 tablespoons onion, grated
1 tablespoon Dijon mustard
1 teaspoon fresh garlic, minced
3 drops hot pepper sauce
1/2 cup fresh parsley, minced
1/2 cup almonds, sliced and toasted
paprika for garnish

Mix cheese, cream, mayonnaise, wine, onion, mustard, garlic and hot pepper sauce in a sauce pan. Fold in crab and 1/4 cup parsley. Heat but do not boil. Spoon into serving dish. Sprinkle with parsley, almonds and paprika.

Serves four.

SPICY CRAB STUFFED MUSHROOMS

1 cup crab meat, flaked
1 pound fresh mushrooms
2 slices wheat bread, crusts removed
4 tablespoons butter
1/4 cup celery, minced
1/4 cup onions, minced
1/4 teaspoon oregano
1/8 teaspoon thyme
1 1/4 teaspoon Worcestershire sauce
1/8 teaspoon salt
1/4 teaspoon pepper
2 drops Tabasco sauce
1 small hot pepper, diced
lemon wedges for garnish
paprika

Remove stems from mushrooms. Place caps in baking dish. Sauté celery and onions in butter. Crumble bread in bowl. Add sauté, spices, crab and two tablespoons melted butter. Mix well.

Stuff mushroom caps with mixture. Sprinkle with paprika. Bake at 350 degrees for 15 minutes. Garnish with lemon wedges.

Serves eight.

TANGY FONDUE CRAB DIP

3/4 pound crab meat, flaked
12 ounces sharp cheddar cheese, grated
8 ounces Monterey Jack cheese, grated
1/3 cup half and half cream
1/2 cup white wine
1 small hot pepper, minced without seeds
1/8 teaspoon rosemary leaves, crushed
sesame sticks or bread cubes

Combine cheeses and milk in top of a double boiler. Place over hot water and stir until cheese melt. Add crab, pepper, wine and rosemary leaves. Blend.

Transfer to chafing dish set on low heat.

Serves three.

THAI CRAB

1 pound crab meat, flaked
1/2 cup unseasoned bread crumbs
1 egg, beaten
1/2 cup mayonnaise
2 tablespoons milk
3 tablespoons Thai chili pepper sauce
4 tablespoons Parmesan cheese
2 tablespoons butter, broken into pieces

Mix all ingredients except cheese and butter. Place mixture in an 8"x8" baking dish. Sprinkle cheese and butter on top. Bake a 350 degrees for 25 minutes until lightly brown on top. Serve hot.
Serves four.

ALASKA STYLE CRAB LOUIS

3 cups cooked crab meat, drained & flaked
1 1/4 cup mayonnaise
3 tablespoons ketchup
dash Tabasco sauce
3 tablespoons olive oil
1 tablespoon wine vinegar
2 tablespoons onion, finely grated
3 tablespoons parsley, finely chopped
1/2 cup heavy cream, whipped
salt to taste
fresh pepper to taste
dash cayenne
6 large tomatoes, sliced
lettuce leaves for garnish
3 hard boiled eggs, sliced for garnish
2 tablespoons stuffed or ripe olives, chopped

Blend mayonnaise, ketchup, Tabasco, oil, vinegar, onion, parsley and whipped cream. Season to taste with salt, pepper and cayenne. Stir in olives. Chill for two hours in refrigerator. Before serving add crab. Place tomatoes on plates and top with crab salad. Garnish with lettuce and egg slices.

Add crab meat to dressing. Serve on salad plates and garnish with lettuce, egg and tomato slices.

Serves five.

BAKED CRAB SALAD

1 pound cooked crab meat, drained & flaked
40 cooked shrimp, shelled and deveined
4 hard boiled eggs, sliced
1/4 cup onion, chopped
1/2 cup green pepper, chopped
1 1/2 cups celery, chopped
1 cup mushroom, sliced
1 cup almonds, sliced
1 (8 ounce) can water chestnuts, drained and sliced
1/2 teaspoon Worcestershire sauce
2 cups mayonnaise
2 cups bread crumbs

Combine all ingredients except bread crumbs. Pour into greased baking dish. Top with bread crumbs Bake at 400° for 25 minutes.
Serves twelve.

CAPTAIN'S CRAB SALAD

1 (4 1/2 ounce) can crab meat, drained & flaked
1 (4 1/2 ounce) can shrimp, drained and rinsed
1 onion, finely chopped
1 green pepper, finely chopped
1 cup celery, chopped
1 cup mayonnaise
1 teaspoon Worcestershire sauce
dash pepper
lemon wedges for garnish

Combine crab, shrimp, onion, pepper and celery. Add mayonnaise, Worcestershire sauce and pepper. Divide between six baking shells. Bake at 350° degrees for 30 minutes. Garnish with lemon wedges.

Serves six.

CHINESE CRAB NOODLE SALAD

1 pound cooked crab meat, drained & flaked
1/2 cup pineapple juice
1/4 cup apple cider vinegar
4 teaspoons soy sauce
1/4 cup rice wine vinegar
pinch of cayenne
4 teaspoons grated fresh ginger
3 cups Chinese cabbage, chopped
4 ounces dry Oriental noodles
1 1/3 cups mung bean sprouts
1/4 cup green onions, sliced
1/4 cup carrots, grated
4 teaspoons cilantro, chopped
2 tablespoons roasted peanuts, chopped

Make dressing by combining juice, vinegars, soy, ginger and cayenne. Mix well and pour into small serving cups. In individual bowls, equally divide and layer cabbage, noodles, sprouts, green onions and crab. Garnish with carrots, cilantro and peanuts. Toss with dressing just before eating.

Serves four.

SALADS

COLD CRAB SALAD

1 pound cooked crab meat, drained & flaked
2 hard boiled eggs, coarsely chopped
1 medium scallion, minced
1 tablespoon pimiento, finely diced
1 tablespoon dill pickle, minced
1 tablespoon small capers, drained
1 tablespoon parsley, minced
1/3 cup mayonnaise
1/4 cup half and half
2 tablespoons Port wine
1 tablespoon Dijon mustard
1/2 teaspoon salt
1/4 teaspoon liquid red pepper
1/8 teaspoon fresh ground pepper
2 tablespoons parsley, minced for garnish
6 pimiento strips for garnish

Combine crab, eggs, scallion, pimiento, pickle, capers and parsley in large bowl. Toss lightly. In small bowl combine cream, Port, mustard, salt, liquid red pepper and black pepper. Pour over crab mixture and toss well. Cover and refrigerate several hours. When ready to serve, spoon crab mixture into six large plates. Garnish with parsley and pimiento strips.
Serves six.

CRAB AND AVOCADO

8 ounces crab meat, flaked
1 avocado, peeled and halved
1/4 cup celery, chopped
2 tablespoons green pepper, chopped
1 tablespoon onion, chopped fine
1/2 teaspoon lemon juice
1/2 teaspoon soy sauce
dash white pepper
1/4 cup mayonnaise
salt to taste
1/3 cup chow mein noodles
lettuce leaves

Toss crab, celery, green pepper and mayonnaise in bowl. Cover and chill. Fold noodles into crab mixture. Spoon salad into avocado. Garnish with celery leaves and place on bed of lettuce.

Serves two.

CRAB AND AVOCADO SALAD WITH NOODLES

1 (8 ounce) can crab meat, drained & flaked
1 avocado, halved
1/4 cup celery, chopped
2 tablespoons green pepper, chopped
1 tablespoon onion, finely chopped
1/2 teaspoon lemon juice
1/2 teaspoon soy sauce
dash white pepper
1/4 cup mayonnaise
salt to taste
1/3 cup chow mein noodles
celery leaves

Toss crab, celery, green pepper, onion, lemon juice, soy sauce, pepper and mayonnaise in bowl. Cover and chill. Fold noodles into crab mixture. Cut the unpeeled avocado in half lengthwise. Remove pit. Brush halves with lemon juice. Sprinkle with salt. Spoon salad into avocado. Garnish with celery leaves and place on bed of lettuce.

Serves two.

CRAB AND EGG SALAD

1 pound cooked crab meat, drained & flaked
4 hard boiled eggs
1/2 cup almonds, sliced and blanched
2 cups heavy cream
1 cup mayonnaise
salt to taste
paprika to taste
1 green pepper, chopped
lettuce leaves

Chop egg whites. Mix crab, egg whites and almonds. Whip cream very stiff and fold into mayonnaise, add salt and paprika to taste. Add to crab mixture. Serve on lettuce. Garnish with pepper and top with riced egg yolks.

CRAB AND PASTA SALAD

8 ounces cooked crab meat, drained & flaked
8 ounces vermicelli, cooked
1/2 cup jicama, chopped coarse
1/4 cup fresh cilantro, chopped
2 medium carrots, shredded
1 medium cucumber, peeled and chopped
1/3 cup mayonnaise
1/3 cup plain yogurt
1 tablespoon soy sauce
1 teaspoon sugar
1/2 teaspoon ground ginger
dash red pepper sauce

Toss vermicelli and vegetables. Mix remaining ingredients and toss with salad.

Serves six.

CRAB, ARTICHOKE AND SHRIMP SALAD

8 ounces cooked crab meat, drained & flaked
1 (4 1/2 ounces) can shrimp, rinsed and drained
6 cups lettuce, torn into bite size pieces
1/2 jar marinated artichoke heats, drained
1/4 cup pitted ripe olives, sliced
1 hard boiled egg, cut into wedges
1/2 teaspoon capers
fresh ground pepper
Italian dressing

Save some crab and shrimp for garnish. Toss remaining crab, shrimp, lettuce, artichoke hearts and olives. Divide between two salad bowls. Garnish with crab, shrimp, egg, capers and pepper. Serve with dressing.

Serves two.

CRAB AVOCADO SALAD

1 pound cooked crab meat, drained & flaked
4 avocados
1/2 cup pecans, chopped
1/2 cup mayonnaise
2 teaspoons ketchup
dash Worcestershire sauce
leaf lettuce
1 cup grapefruit sections
2 hard boiled eggs, chopped
black olives for garnish

Cut avocados in half and remove seeds. Combine crab with next four ingredients. Spoon into avocados. Serve on a bed of lettuce with grapefruit sections. Garnish with eggs and olives.

Serves four.

CRAB LOUIS

1 pound cooked crab meat, drained & flaked
1 head lettuce, shredded
1/2 teaspoon salt
4 tomatoes, sliced
1 cucumber, peeled and sliced
3 hard boiled eggs, sliced
1 cup mayonnaise
1/4 cup chili sauce
2 tablespoons chives, chopped
1 tablespoon lemon juice
dash Worcestershire sauce
capers

Place lettuce in a large chilled salad bowl. Sprinkle with salt. Mound crab in center and surround with tomato, cucumber and egg.

Combine remaining ingredients. Spoon over crab and garnish with capers.

Serves four.

CRAB SALAD

1 pound cooked crab meat, drained & flaked
1 cup celery, chopped
1/2 cup green pepper, finely chopped
4 hard boiled eggs, chopped
1/4 cup onion, finely chopped
juice of 1 lemon
3 tablespoons relish
mayonnaise
salt to taste
lettuce leaves for garnish
parsley for garnish
lemon wedges for garnish

Toss all ingredients together with just enough mayonnaise to bind mixture. Let salad stand in refrigerator two hours. Season to taste. Garnish.
Serves four.

CRAB AND SHRIMP SALAD

3/4 pound cooked crab meat, drained & flaked
3/4 pound cooked shrimp, shelled and deveined
1 head romaine lettuce, torn into bite size pieces
1 red onion, thinly sliced
1/2 cup radishes, thinly sliced
1 green pepper, diced
2 stalks celery, diced
1/2 cut black olives, pitted
4 anchovies
ranch style creamy onion dressing

In a large bowl, toss lettuce and arrange remaining ingredients over lettuce. Top with dressing and serve.
Serves four.

SALADS

CURRIED CRAB RICE SALAD

6 ounces cooked crab meat, drained & flaked
1 cup long grain rice, cooked
3 tablespoons butter
1/2 cup onion, finely chopped
1/3 cup celery, diced
1/3 cup green pepper, diced
1 tablespoon curry powder
1/2 cup cream
salt to taste
fresh ground pepper
fresh parsley
lemon slices for garnish

Sauté onion, celery and green pepper in butter for 3 minutes. Stir in curry powder and cook until vegetables are tender but still crisp. Remove from heat and stir vegetables into rice. Add crab meat and toss together.

Just before serving, season heavy cream with salt and whip gently. It must not be stiff. Season salad with pepper and parsley. Fold in whipped cream. Garnish with lemons.

Serves four.

EASY CRAB SALAD

1 1/2 cup cooked crab meat, drained & flaked
2 cups macaroni, cooked
2/3 cup mayonnaise
1 tablespoon chili sauce
3 Italian roma tomatoes, quartered
1/3 cup small ripe olives, pitted
4 ounces salad green coarsely chopped

Mix mayonnaise and chili sauce in large bowl. Add macaroni, tomatoes and olives. Toss. Add salad greens and crab. Toss.
Serves four.

HOT CRAB SALAD

1 pound cooked crab meat, drained & flaked
2 cups celery, chopped
1/2 cup almonds, slivered
2 teaspoon onion, chopped
1 cup mayonnaise
2 tablespoons lemon juice
1 cup potato chips, crushed
1/2 cup sharp Cheddar cheese, shredded

Combine all ingredients except chips and cheese, and put in buttered casserole. Sprinkle chips and cheese on top. Bake at 400° for 25 minutes. Serve hot.
Serves six.

KING CRAB SALAD

1 1/2 pounds cooked king crab meat, drained & flaked
2 (10 ounce) packages frozen peas, cooked,
**   drained & chilled**
2 cups celery, sliced
2 cups mayonnaise
2 teaspoons lemon juice
2 teaspoons horseradish, grated
1/2 teaspoon curry powder
1 teaspoon salt
salad greens

Mix celery, mayonnaise, lemon juice, horseradish, curry powder and salt. Combine all ingredients and serve on salad greens.

Serves twelve.

KING CRAB AND SPINACH SALAD

12 ounces cooked king crab meat, drained & flaked
1 (10 ounce) package frozen chopped spinach,
      cooked, drained & chilled
1 cup mayonnaise
1 tablespoon lemon juice
1 teaspoon dry mustard
1/2 teaspoon horseradish, grated

  At serving time mix spinach, mayonnaise, lemon juice,
mustard and horseradish. Toss lightly with crab.
  Serves six.

MOLDED CRAB SALAD SUPREME

1 cup cooked crab meat, drained & flaked
1 (10 ounce) can cream of shrimp soup
3 ounces cream cheese, softened
1 package unflavored gelatin
1/2 cup cold water
2 tablespoons parsley, chopped
2 tablespoons celery, minced
1 tablespoon lemon rind, grated
salad greens

Gradually blend soup with softened cream cheese.

Sprinkle one package gelatin and water. Place over low heat and stir until gelatin dissolved. Remove from heat. Blend in soup mixture, crab, parsley, celery and lemon rind. Pour into a 1 1/2 quart mold and chill until firm. Remove mold and serve on salad greens.

Serves six.

QUICK CRAB SALAD

8 ounces cooked crab meat, drained & flaked
1 avocado, peeled and halved
Thousand Island dressing
lettuce leaves

Mix crab and dressing together. Place avocado on a bed of lettuce and stuff with crab mixture.
Serves two.

BUTTERMILK BISQUE

1 pound crab meat, flaked
1 onion, chopped
2 tablespoons carrot, minced
1 tablespoon fresh parsley, minced
2 tablespoons butter
1 teaspoon curry powder
2 cucumbers, peeled and chopped
2 bottles clam juice
6 cups chilled buttermilk
2 teaspoon salt
dash pepper
lemon juice
sour cream for garnish
paprika for garnish

Sauté in butter onion, carrot and parsley. Add curry powder and cucumber. Cook two minutes. Blend crab and clam juice until smooth. Pour into bowl and add buttermilk. Season with salt and pepper. Add lemon juice as needed. Chill four hours. Top each serving with sour cream and paprika.
Serves six.

COLD CRAB GUMBO

1 (7 1/2 ounces) can crab meat, flaked
1/2 cup onion, diced
1/2 cup celery, diced
1/2 cup green pepper, diced
1/2 cup leeks, diced
2 tablespoons butter
1 quart chicken broth
1 cup stewed tomatoes, chopped
1 cup okra, sliced
1 bay leaf
1 teaspoon salt
1/4 teaspoon pepper

Sauté in butter onion, celery, green pepper and leeks in large pan. Add broth, tomatoes, okra and bay leaf. Season with salt and pepper. Simmer 40 minutes. Cool uncovered. Refrigerate. Skim of fat. Before serving add crab. Serve soup cold.

Serves six.

CRAB

COLD CRAB SOUP

8 ounces crab meat, flaked
3 tablespoons butter
2 tablespoons flour
1/2 teaspoon curry
1 teaspoon salt
4 cups milk
1/4 cup white wine
1 cup sour cream
fresh chives, chopped for garnish

Melt butter in sauce pan. Blend in flour, curry and salt. Add milk Cook and stir until thick and bubbly. Add crab and wine. Heat. Cool. Blend 1/2 cup of the soup with sour cream until smooth. Stir mixture into soup. Chill for several hours. Garnish with chives.

Serves eight.

CRAB AND MUSHROOM STEW

1 pound crab meat, flaked
1 pound mushrooms, sliced
2 green onions, chopped
2 cloves garlic, minced
5 tablespoons butter
1 tablespoon whiskey
1 cup half and half cream
3 cups rice, cooked
1/4 cup parsley, chopped
salt to taste
pepper to taste

Sauté in butter mushrooms, onions and garlic. Season with salt and pepper. Remove mixture from pan and keep warm. Add whiskey. Add crab and mix for one minute. Return mushrooms to pan. Stir in cream and heat until hot.

Mix rice with parsley and pack into an unbuttered five cup ring mold. Turn it out on a warm platter. Spoon crab mixture into center and serve.

Serves four.

CRAB

CRAB AND TOFU SOUP

3/4 pound crab meat, flaked
1/2 package tofu, cubed
2 tablespoons oil
1/2 cup green onion, chopped
1 clove garlic, minced
1 teaspoon ginger, grated
3 cans chicken broth
2 fresh mushrooms, sliced
2 tablespoons dry sherry
salt to taste
pepper to taste

Sauté onion, garlic, ginger and tofu in oil. Add broth and mushrooms and bring to a boil. Stir in crab and sherry. Simmer three minutes. Season.

Serves four.

CRAB BISQUE

1 (7 1/2 ounce) can crab meat, flaked and drained
1 (10 1/2 ounce) can cream of asparagus soup
1 (10 1/2 ounce) can cream of mushroom soup
2 1/2 cups milk
1 cup cream
1/3 cup sherry

Blend soups in large pot. Gradually stir in milk and cream. Heat to just boiling. Add crab and heat. Add sherry and serve topped with butter.

Garnish with parsley.

Serves six.

CRAB BISQUE WITH YAMS

1/2 pound crab meat
2 tablespoons butter
4 tablespoon onion, chopped fine
1 1/2 teaspoons flour
1 1/2 cups white wine
1/4 teaspoon paprika
4 cups milk
1 1/2 pounds yams, boiled, peeled and cubed
salt to taste
cayenne to taste
1/2 pint cream
3 drops Tabasco
fresh nutmeg for garnish

Sauté in butter onion in a large pot. Add flour, blend with a whisk and cook for five minutes. Whisk in wine, and paprika. Cook a few minutes. Add milk, yams, salt and cayenne to taste. Bring to a boil. Stir occasionally. Simmer for five minutes. Drain through a colander, reserve all liquid.

Cool solids for a few minutes and then puree in a food processor. Blend puree into reserved liquid. Set over low heat and add crab and cream. Stir constantly. Simmer soup for ten minutes. Season to taste with Tabasco and nutmeg. Serve in soup bowls.

Serves six.

CRAB CHOWDER

2 pounds crab, flaked
2 (7 ounce) cans clams, minced, do not drain
2 tablespoons oil
2 large onions, chopped
3 shallots, chopped
6 cloves garlic, minced
1 (16 ounce) can tomatoes, chopped
3 cups tomato juice
1 tablespoon dry parsley
1 teaspoon dry thyme
1 teaspoon dry basil
2 teaspoons sugar
3 threads saffron
1/2 teaspoon turmeric
1/4 teaspoon red pepper
1 pound potatoes, sliced
salt to taste
pepper to taste

Combine all ingredients except crab and clams. Simmer 20 minutes. Add clams with juice. Simmer for five minutes. Bring to boil and add crab. Cook for five minutes. Serve in soup bowls with fresh bread.

Serves six.

CRAB

CRAB CIOPPINO

2 Dungeness crabs, cleaned and cracked
1 pound cooked shrimp, shelled and deveined
12 clams in thin shell for steaming, scrubbed
1/4 cup oil
1 large onion, chopped
2 cloves garlic, minced
1 large green pepper, chopped and seeded
1/3 cup fresh parsley, chopped
1 (15 ounce) can tomato sauce
1 (28 ounce) can tomatoes
1 bay leaf
1 cup white wine
1 teaspoon dry basil
1/2 teaspoon oregano leaves

Combine oil, onion, garlic, green pepper and parsley. Cook until onion is soft. Stir in tomato sauce, tomatoes, wine, bay leaf, basil and oregano. Cover and simmer 20 minutes until thickened.

Add clams, crab and shrimp. Cover and simmer gently until clams pop open and shrimp turn pink. Serve in soup bowls.

Serves six.

CRAB GUMBO

8 ounces crab meat, flaked
1/2 cup onion, chopped
1/2 cup celery, chopped
1 clove garlic, minced
1/4 cup butter
1/4 teaspoon dry thyme
2 tablespoons salt
1/4 teaspoon sugar
1 bay leaf
dash pepper
1 (10 ounce) frozen package okra, sliced
2 (20 ounce) cans tomatoes
1 1/2 cup rice, cooked

Sauté in butter onion, celery and garlic in large pan. Add seasonings, okra and tomatoes. Cover and simmer 45 minutes. Remove bay leaf. Add crab and heat. Serve over rice.
Serves six.

CRAB JAMBALAYA

1 pound crab meat
1/2 cup bacon chopped
1/2 cup onion, chopped
1/2 cup celery, chopped
1/2 cup green pepper, chopped
1 (29 ounce) can tomatoes, chopped
3/4 cup rice
1 tablespoons Worcestershire sauce
1/2 teaspoon salt
dash pepper

Fry in large pot bacon. Add onion, celery and green pepper. Cook until tender. Add tomatoes, rice and seasoning. Simmer covered for 25 minutes until rice is tender. Add crab meat and heat.

Serves six.

CRAB SOUP

1 pound crab meat, flaked
1 cube vegetable bouillon
1 cup water, boiling
1/3 cup onion, chopped
1/4 cup butter, melted
2 tablespoons flour
1 clove garlic, chopped fine
1/2 teaspoon celery salt
1 quart half and half cream
salt to taste
pepper to taste
fresh parsley for garnish
tomato slice for garnish

Dissolve bouillon in water and blend. Sauté onion in butter until translucent. Blend in flour, garlic and celery slat. Add cream and bouillon gradually. Blend carefully. Stir and cook until thickened. Add crab. Stir and simmer until heated. Salt and pepper to taste. Garnish.

Serves four.

CRAB SOUP WITH BEER

1/2 pound crab meat, flaked
1 can tomato soup
1 can pea soup
1 can beer
1 cup milk
dash Worcestershire sauce
salt to taste
pepper to taste

Combine all ingredients into a pot and heat. Do not boil.
Serves four.

CRAB STEW

**1/2 cup crab meat, flaked
1 1/2 pounds halibut, cubed
1/2 cup celery, diced
1 small onion, chopped
1 carrot , chopped
1 large potato, diced
1/2 teaspoon garlic salt
flour for thickening
salt to taste**

Place vegetables in sauce pan. Barely cover with water and boil for 15 minutes. Add halibut, crab and garlic. Simmer ten minutes. Thicken with flour paste. Salt to taste. Mix well.
Serves four.

EASY CRAB BISQUE

8 ounces crab meat, flaked
1 can cream of tomato soup
1 can pea sour
2 1/2 cups milk
1 cup cream
1/4 cup sherry
1/4 cup sour cream
salt to taste
dillweed, minced for garnish

Heat in large sauce pan tomato soup, pea sour, milk and cream. Sir in crab and sherry. Heat. Do not boil. Serve with cream and dillweed on top for garnish.

Serves four.

HOMER CRAB SOUP

1 1/2 pounds crab meat, flaked
2 tablespoon shallots, finely chopped
1/3 cup sherry
3 tablespoons paprika
2 pinches thyme
4 cups bottled clam juice
2 cups heavy cream
2 teaspoons cornstarch
1/2 teaspoon cayenne pepper
salt to taste
pepper to taste

Combine shallots and sherry in large saucepan. Simmer until reduced in half. Add crab, paprika and thyme. Simmer for three minutes. Add juice and cream. Bring to a boil.

Dissolve cornstarch in one teaspoon water and whisk into soup. Simmer for five minutes. Season to taste.

Serves four.

JUNEAU CRAB SOUP

8 ounce crab meat, flaked
2 tablespoons butter
1 tablespoon flour
2 cups water
1 onion, chopped
1 stalk celery, chopped
1 sprig fresh parsley, chopped
pinch of thyme
2 drops Tabasco sauce
3 cups milk, scalded
salt to taste
pepper to taste

Melt butter in sauce pan. Add flour and brown. Stir in water. Add crab, vegetables and seasonings. Simmer for 30 minutes. Pour in milk. Season and serve.

Serves four.

KODIAK STYLE CIOPPINO

2 Dungeness crabs, cleaned and cracked
18 steamer clams
12 raw shrimp, shelled and deveined
1 large onion, chopped
6 cloves garlic, minced
6 tablespoons olive oil
1 green pepper, diced
2 stalks celery, finely chopped
1/3 cup fresh parsley, minced
2 cup tomatoes, chopped and peeled
1 (6 ounce) can tomato paste
2 cups water
1 bottle red wine
1 teaspoon oregano
1/2 teaspoon dry thyme
1/2 teaspoon pepper
1 bay leaf
salt to taste
pepper to taste

Sauté in large pot onion and garlic in olive oil. Add green peppers, celery, parsley, tomatoes, tomato paste, water, wine and spices. Simmer covered for 45 minutes until celery is soft.

Bring sauce to a boil. Add crab and clams. Return to a boil. Simmer ten minutes. Add shrimp and simmer ten minutes until clams open and shrimp are pink. Season to taste. Serve with sourdough bread.

Serves six.

NEW ORLEANS CRAB GUMBO

1 pound crab meat, flaked
4 slices bacon, fried crisp and broken into bits
2 cups okra, sliced
3 tablespoons butter
1 onion, chopped
1 clove garlic, minced
1 green pepper, chopped
1 stalk celery, chopped
2 tomatoes, chopped and peeled
pinch dry thyme
1 quart hot water
salt to taste
pepper to taste

Sauté in butter okra, onion, garlic, pepper and celery in a large pan. Add tomatoes, thyme, water, salt and pepper. Simmer covered 30 minutes. Add crab and simmer ten minutes. Garnish with bacon bits.
Serves six.

SEWARD STYLE CIOPPINO

2 Dungeness crabs, cleaned and cracked
12 clams for steaming, scrubbed
2 pounds salmon fillets, cubed
1/4 cup butter
2 medium onions, chopped
2 cloves garlic, minced
1/3 cup fresh parsley, chopped
2 (14 1/2 ounce) cans chicken broth
1 cup water
1 1/2 cups white wine
1 bay leaf
1/2 teaspoon dry thyme leaves
1/2 teaspoon dry rosemary

Sauté in 8 quart pan in butter onion, garlic and parsley. Add broth, water, wine, bay leaf, thyme and rosemary. Cover and simmer 15 minutes.

Add crab, clams and salmon. Cover and simmer for 15 minutes until clams pop open. Serve in soup bowls.

Serves six.

SITKA CRAB STEW

1 pound crab meat, flaked
2 tablespoons butter
2 cups milk
2 cups half and half cream
2 drops Tabasco sauce
1 teaspoon Worcestershire sauce
6 tablespoons port wine
4 lemon slices
salt to taste
pepper to taste
fresh parsley, chopped for garnish

Combine in sauce pan milk, crab and butter. Simmer 10 minutes. Add cream and seasonings. Bring to near boil. Stir gently. Remove from heat and add wine.

Serve in soup bowls topped with lemon and parsley.

Serves four.

BROILED CRAB SANDWICHES

1 cup cooked crab meat, drained & flaked
1 cup Swiss cheese, shredded
1/2 cup mayonnaise
1 green onion, thinly sliced
4 slices whole grain bread, toasted
alfalfa sprouts

Mix all ingredients except toast and sprouts. Arrange sprouts on toast and top with crab mixture.

Place sandwiches on cookie sheet. Broil until mixture is hot and bubbly.

Serves four.

CRAB AND CHICKEN OVER TOAST

8 ounces cooked crab meat, drained & flaked
1 1/2 cups cooked chicken, diced
3 tablespoons butter
3 tablespoons flour
1/2 teaspoon salt
1/2 teaspoon paprika
1/8 teaspoon nutmeg
1 cup chicken broth
1 cup sour cream
6 drops Tabasco sauce
1/8 teaspoon garlic powder
4 slices bacon, cooked and crumbled
1 (10 ounce) package frozen green peas,
**   cooked and drained**
4 slices toast, buttered

Melt butter in sauce pan. Add flour and seasonings. Cook over low heat, stirring until mixture is smooth and bubbly. Remove from heat. Stir in chicken broth. Heat to boiling, stirring constantly. Boil one minute. Remove form heat. Slowly stir in cream, Tabasco and garlic. Add chicken, crab and bacon. Heat and stir constantly. Pour mixture in serving dish. Arrange hot peas around edge of dish. Serve over toast.

Serves four.

CRAB AND ENGLISH MUFFINS

6 ounces cooked crab meat, drained & flaked
2 English muffins, split, toasted and buttered
3 tablespoons mayonnaise
fresh lemon juice to taste
salt to taste
fresh ground pepper to taste
1 large tomato, sliced
4 slices Swiss cheese

Toss crab with mayonnaise and lemon juice. Salt and pepper to taste. Spread over muffin halves. Top with tomato and cheese. Broil until cheese is bubbly.

Serves two.

CRAB CHEESE BURGERS

1 pound cooked crab meat, drained & flaked
1 pound sharp Cheddar cheese, grated
1 1/2 cups onion, minced
1 green pepper, minced
1/2 cup celery, minced
1 small can black olives, chopped
1/2 cup oil
four hamburger buns

Mix first seven ingredients. Refrigerate overnight.
Spoon mixture onto hamburger buns. Wrap in foil. Bake at 300° for 50 minutes.
Serves four.

CRAB LOAF

1 pound cooked crab meat, drained & flaked
1 long loaf French bread
mayonnaise
lemon juice
1 avocado, sliced
tomato, sliced

Split French loaf lengthwise and spread with mayonnaise. Top with crab. Cover with mayonnaise thinned with lemon juice. Put top in place and cut into four sandwiches. Serve with avocado and tomatoes.
Serves four.

CRAB

CREAMED CRAB

1 pound cooked crab meat, drained & flaked
2 tablespoons butter
2 tablespoons flour
1 cup cream
2 hard boiled eggs, chopped
1/2 teaspoon salt
1/2 teaspoon pepper
1 teaspoon paprika
dash cayenne
1 teaspoon sherry
4 slices toast

Melt butter in pan and add flour. Stir until smooth. Add cream, eggs and seasonings. Cook until thick. Add crab. Remove from heat and stir in sherry. Serve over toast.
Serves four.

SPAGHETTI WITH CRAB SAUCE

1 pound crab meat, flaked
4 cloves garlic, minced
1/2 cup butter
2 tablespoon olive oil
1 cup green onion, sliced
2 medium tomatoes, diced
1/2 cup parsley, chopped
2 tablespoons lemon juice
1/2 teaspoon Italian dressing
1/2 teaspoon salt
1 pound spaghetti, cooked

Sauté garlic in butter and oil. Add remaining ingredients except spaghetti. Simmer for ten minutes. Toss spaghetti with crab mixture. Serve with grated Parmesan cheese.

Serves six.

ASPARAGUS AND CRAB

1 pound crab meat, flaked
2 egg yolks
3 tablespoons lemon juice
1 tablespoon tomato paste
1 teaspoon Dijon mustard
salt to taste
1/2 teaspoon fresh ground pepper
1 1/4 cups oil
2 pounds asparagus, trimmed, steamed, cooled and dried
1 tablespoon shallot, minced fine

    In medium bowl whisk yolks, lemon juice, paste, mustard, salt and pepper.
    Gradually whisk in oil. Mayonnaise will thicken.
    Fold mayonnaise, crab and shallot. Arrange asparagus on plate. Spoon crab mayonnaise over center of asparagus.
    Serves four.

AVOCADOS STUFFED WITH CRAB

1 pound crab meat, flaked
2 tablespoons butter
2 tablespoons flour
1 cup milk
1/4 teaspoon salt
dash of pepper
1/4 teaspoon Worcestershire
2 tablespoons pimento, chopped
2 tablespoons olives, chopped
3 avocados, cut in half
1/4 cup cheese, grated

Melt butter and blend in flour. Add milk and cook until thick and smooth. Add seasonings, pimento, olives and crab. fill avocado center with crab mixture. Top with cheese. Bake at 350 degrees for 25 minutes until brown.
Serves six.

BRISTOL BAY CRAB IMPERIAL

2 pounds crab meat, flaked
1/2 cup mayonnaise
2 teaspoons pimento, chopped
1 teaspoon Worcestershire sauce
6 drops Tabasco sauce
6 tablespoons mayonnaise for topping
paprika for garnish

Combine mayonnaise, pimento, Worcestershire and Tabasco sauce. Pour over crab and mix lightly. Place in six custard cups. Top each with mayonnaise. Sprinkle with paprika. Bake at 350 degrees for 25 minutes until brown.
Serves six.

CAJUN CRAB AND NOODLES

6 ounces crab meat, flaked
3 cups noodles, cooked and drained
1 tablespoon oil
3/4 cup green pepper, chopped
1 medium onion, chopped
2 tablespoons fresh parsley, chopped
1/8 teaspoon cayenne pepper
2 cloves garlic, minced
1/8 teaspoon pepper
1 tablespoon flour
1 (16 ounce) can whole tomatoes, chopped
1 (10 ounce) package frozen okra, chopped
1 (6 ounce) can shrimp, drained

Sauté in oil green pepper, onion, parsley, red pepper and garlic. Stir in flour and tomatoes.

Cook uncovered and stir frequently until thick and boils. Stir in okra, shrimp and crab. Cook five minutes. Serve over noodles.

Serves six.

CARIBBEAN CRAB SOUFFLE

1/2 pound crab meat, flaked
1/2 cup unsweetened coconut, shredded
4 tablespoons unsalted butter
1/3 cup celery, minced
1 clove garlic, minced
1/2 teaspoon curry powder
1/2 teaspoon dried thyme
1/2 teaspoon dried red pepper
1/2 teaspoon salt
fresh ground pepper to taste
3 tablespoons flour
1 1/4 cups milk
4 egg yolks
6 egg whites
1/4 teaspoon lemon juice

Set aside a buttered 8 cup souffle dish.

Place a small nonstick skillet on low heat and toast the coconut five minutes. Set aside. Melt butter and add celery, garlic, curry powder, thyme, pepper, salt and pepper. Cook three minutes. Add flour and stir until smooth. Cook one minute. Add milk and cook over medium heat until mixtures boils and thickens. Set aside and cool.

Whisk yolks one at a time into sauce. Stir in crab and coconut. Beat egg whites and lemon juice until frothy. Beat until stiff. Stir in one forth of the egg whites into crab mixture. Place into the souffle dish. Bake at 400 degrees for 30 minutes until brown.

Serves eight.

COOK INLET CRAB AND SHRIMP CAKES

1 cup crab meat, flaked
1 cup cooked shrimp, shelled and deveined
1 egg
1 egg white
1 teaspoon dill weed
2 tablespoons Worcestershire
1/2 teaspoon dry mustard
1 cup bread crumbs
1 cup red pepper, diced
1/4 cup mayonnaise
2 tablespoons green onion, diced
1 1/2 tablespoons butter, melted
lemon wedges for garnish

Beat eggs and egg white. Add dill, Worcestershire, mustard, crab, shrimp, crumbs, pepper, mayonnaise and onion. Shape in 12 patties 1/2 inch thick.

Fry in butter until golden. Drain on paper towels. Garnish. Serves four.

CRAB ALASKA

1 1/2 pounds crab meat, flaked
1/3 cup lemon juice
3/4 cup butter, melted
paprika for garnish

Pour butter and lemon over crab and toss. Place in six custard cup. Garnish.

Bake at 450 degrees for 15 minutes until brown.

Serves six.

CRAB ALMONDINE

1 pound crab meat, flaked
1/2 cup almond, slivered
2 tablespoons oil
1 teaspoon fresh dill, minced
2 tablespoons fresh parsley, minced
1 green onion, sliced
4 tablespoons butter
1/4 cup Cognac
1/4 cup cream
2 cups rice, cooked
salt to taste
pepper to taste

Mix almonds in oil in a frying pan. Bake at 350 degrees until golden.

Remove from oven. Stir in dill, parsley and salt. Set aside

Sauté in butter onions. Add crab and cook until hot. Sprinkle with Cognac and set aflame. After flame stops, stir in cream. Simmer two minutes. Season. Place crab on a warm plate. Spoon almonds over. Serve with rice.

Serves four.

CRAB AND ARTICHOKE CASSEROLE

3/4 pound crab meat, flaked
1 1/2 cups artichoke hearts, cooked
3 tablespoons butter
1/2 pound mushrooms, sliced
3 tablespoons flour
3/4 cup milk
3/4 cup chicken broth
1 tablespoon Worcestershire
1/4 cup sherry
pepper to taste
1/2 cup fresh Parmesan cheese, grated
2 tablespoons fresh parsley, chopped for garnish

Place artichoke in buttered 2 quart baking dish. Top with crab.

Sauté mushrooms in butter. Add flour and stir until bubbly. Remove from heat. Gradually add milk and broth and stir constantly. Return to heat and cook until sauce thickens. Stir in sherry and Worcestershire. Season.

Pour sauce over crab and sprinkle with cheese. Bake at 375 degrees for 20 minutes until bubbly.

Serves four.

CRAB AND CHEDDAR QUICHE

1 1/2 cups crab meat
9 inch pastry shell
1 egg white
1 cup Cheddar cheese, grated
2 green onions, chopped
2 tablespoons parsley, chopped
3 eggs, beaten
1 cup half and half cream
2 tablespoons sherry
1/2 teaspoon lemon rind, grated
1/2 teaspoon salt
1/4 teaspoon pepper
pinch cayenne
paprika for garnish

Brush shell with egg white. Sprinkle in cheese, crab, onions and parsley in layers. Mix eggs, cream, sherry, lemon, cayenne, salt and pepper. Pour into shell. Sprinkle with paprika. Bake at 325 degrees for 45 minutes until center is done.

Serves four.

CRAB AND PARMESAN QUICHE

8 ounces crab meat
1 nine inch cooked pie shell
1/2 cup green onion, chopped
1 (2 ounce) can mushroom, drained
2 tablespoons butter
4 eggs, beaten
1 1/2 cups half and half cream
2 tablespoons parsley, chopped
1/2 teaspoon salt
1/8 teaspoon pepper
1/4 cup Parmesan cheese, grated
paprika for garnish

Sauté in butter onion and mushrooms. Combine with crab, egg, cream, parsley, salt and pepper. Pour into shell and top with cheese. Sprinkle with paprika. Bake at 450 degrees for 45 minutes until done in center.

Serves six.

CRAB AND RICE

3 cups crab meat, flaked
8 tablespoons butter
4 cloves garlic, minced
1 package artichoke hearts, thawed and drained
2 1/2 cups rice, cooked
salt to taste
pepper to taste
2 tablespoons parsley, chopped for garnish

Sauté in a skillet butter and crab. Add garlic and artichokes. Stir until coated. Add rice and stir until hot. Season and garnish.

Serves six.

CRAB AND SHRIMP CASSEROLE

8 ounces crab meat
1 pound cooked shrimp, shelled and deveined
1 (10 ounce) can shrimp soup
1 (10 ounce) can Newburg sauce
4 scallions, chopped
1 (8 ounce) can black olives, chopped
1 can pimentos, chopped
1 clove garlic, minced
1/2 cup sherry
2 (3 ounce) cans mushrooms, drained
1 can water chestnuts, drained and sliced
1 teaspoon sugar
3/4 teaspoon salt
1/4 teaspoon white pepper
Parmesan cheese for topping

    Toss in 6 quart casserole all ingredients. Top with cheese. Bake uncovered at 350 degrees for 50 minutes.
    Serves six.

CRAB CASSEROLE WITH MUSHROOMS

1 pound crab meat, flaked
2 tablespoons butter
1 cup mushrooms, chopped
1 tablespoon flour
1/2 cup cream
juice of 1/2 lemon
1 teaspoon capers, drained
1 teaspoon parsley, chopped
2 egg whites, beaten stiff

Sauté mushrooms in butter. Stir in flour. Cook for two minutes, then add cream.

Stir until thickened, Add crab, lemon, capers and egg. Place in buttered casserole. Bake at 350 degrees for 20 minutes.

Serves six.

CRAB CASSEROLE WITH TOMATOES

1 pound crab meat, flaked
1 small green pepper, chopped
1/4 cup onion, chopped
2 tablespoons butter, melted
1/2 cup mushrooms, sliced
1/4 cup flour
3 tablespoons butter, melted
1 1/2 cups milk
1/2 cup white wine
1/2 teaspoon salt
1/8 teaspoon pepper
1 medium tomato, peeled and chopped
1/2 cup Parmesan cheese, grated

Sauté in butter (two tablespoons), onion and green pepper. Add mushroom and sauté. Combine in sauce pan butter (three tablespoons) and flour. Heat for three minutes. Gradually add milk and cook until thickened. Combine crab, sauté mixture and sauce into a buttered casserole. Season. Top with tomatoes and cheese. Bake at 350 degrees for 45 minutes.

Serves four.

CRAB COQUILLES

1 pound crab meat, flaked
2 eggs, beaten
1 teaspoon salt
1/4 teaspoon pepper
1/2 teaspoon dry mustard
1 green onion, chopped
2 tablespoons green pepper, chopped fine
2 tablespoons parsley, minced
1/3 cup mayonnaise
1 teaspoon horseradish
paprika for garnish

Mix all ingredients except crab and paprika. Spoon mixture into six baking dishes. Garnish. Bake at 350 degrees for 20 minutes.

Serves six.

CRAB CREPES

12 ounces crab meat, flaked
3/4 cup flour
1/2 teaspoon salt
2 eggs, beaten
1 cup milk
1 teaspoon butter, melted
2 tablespoons butter
1/2 teaspoon Tabasco
1/4 teaspoon Worcestershire
1/2 teaspoon dry mustard
1/2 teaspoon salt
1 cup evaporated milk
2 tablespoons Parmesan cheese
1 tablespoon sherry

Blend flour, salt, eggs and milk until smooth. Add melted butter and blend. Let stand several hours. Heat a five inch skillet. Use two tablespoons crepe batter for each crepe. Spread evenly by tilting pan. Brown crepe. Remove and keep warm. Repeat process for each crepe.

Melt butter. Add flour, Tabasco, Worcestershire, mustard and salt. Blend. Add milk and stir until thick. Remove from heat. Stir in cheese, cream and sherry. Add 1/4 cup of sauce to crab. Place three tablespoons of crab into crepe. Roll up and place in shallow baking dish. Thin remaining sauce and spoon over crepes. Bake at 400 degrees for 12 minutes.

Serves six.

CRAB FRITTATA

6 ounces crab meat, flaked
4 ounces mushrooms, sliced
4 green onions, sliced
1/4 cup butter
8 eggs, beaten
1/2 teaspoon lemon and pepper seasoning
1 cup Fontina cheese, shredded
1 tablespoon fresh basil, chopped
2 tablespoons Parmesan cheese, grated

Sauté in skillet mushrooms and onions in butter. Stir in crab. Season eggs and stir in Fontina cheese and basil. Pour over crab. Cover and cook ten minutes until set and brown on bottom.

Broil frittatas two minutes until brown. Sprinkle with Parmesan cheese and cut in wedges.

CRAB IMPERIAL

1 pound crab meat, flaked
2 stalks celery, minced
1/3 cup mayonnaise
1 teaspoon fresh lemon juice
1/4 teaspoon Accent
2 dashes Worcestershire sauce
1/2 teaspoon garlic powder
cracker crumbs
Parmesan cheese

Butter casserole dish. Combine all ingredients except cracker crumbs and cheese. Mix well. Refrigerate one hour. Place in casserole dish. Top with crumbs and cheese and butter dots. Bake at 350 degrees for 20 minutes.

Serves four.

CRAB LAYER

8 ounces crab meat, flaked
6 ounces plain croutons
1 1/2 cups Swiss cheese, shredded
6 green onions, sliced
1 1/2 cup milk
1/2 teaspoon dry mustard
4 eggs

Arrange half of croutons in buttered square baking dish. Layer with cheese, crab, onions and remaining croutons. Beat milk, mustard and eggs. Pour over croutons. Cover and refrigerate two hours.

Bake uncovered at 300 degrees for 60 minutes until center is done. Let stand ten minutes before cutting.

Serves six.

CRAB OMELET

2 tablespoons crab meat
1 1/2 teaspoons butter
2 tablespoons onion, chopped
2 tablespoons tomato, chopped
2 tablespoons green pepper, chopped
2 eggs
1 tablespoon water
1/4 teaspoon salt
1 1/2 teaspoons butter

Sauté in skillet crab, onion, tomato and pepper in butter. Set aside.

Beat eggs, water and salt. Pour into omelet pan hot with bubbly butter. When the omelet is set, spoon in crab mixture on half of the omelet and fold. Heat and serve.

Serves one.

CRAB OMELET WITH SPROUTS

1 cup crab meat, flaked
2 green onions, sliced
1 1/4 cups fresh bean sprouts
1/2 cup mushrooms, sliced
4 eggs
1/2 teaspoon salt
1/8 teaspoon pepper
1/8 teaspoon garlic powder
2 tablespoons oil for frying
1/2 cup chicken broth
1 teaspoon soy sauce
1/4 teaspoon sugar
1 teaspoon sherry
1 teaspoon cornstarch
1 tablespoon water

Make sauce by combining last six ingredients in pan. Stir over low heat until thickened. Set aside.

In a large bowl add crab, onion, sprouts and mushroom. Beat eggs, salt, pepper and garlic. Mix with crab.

Heat a large skillet with oil to cover bottom. Spoon in 1/4 of egg mixture. Cook until set and brown. Turn over and cook other side. Repeat for other omelets. Serve with hot sauce over top.

Serves four.

CRAB OMELETS

1 pound crab meat, flaked
2 cups half and half cream
2 tablespoons green onion, sliced
1/2 teaspoon thyme
1/2 teaspoon salt
1/8 teaspoon hot pepper sauce
2 tablespoons flour
1/4 cup water
12 eggs
1 1/2 teaspoons salt
1/8 teaspoon pepper
1/4 cup butter
1 1/2 cups Cheddar cheese, grated

Combine crab, cream, onion, thyme, teaspoon salt and hot pepper. Cook until hot. Combine flour and water. Mix well. Add to crab mixture and stir constantly.

For each omelet beat two eggs, 1/4 teaspoon salt and pepper. Pour mixture into hot omelet pan with bubbly butter. When egg is almost done, sprinkle with 1/4 cup cheese on top. Cook until cheese melts. Place 1/2 crab mixture on one side of omelet. Fold in half and heat. Repeat for each omelet.

Serves six.

CRAB PANCAKE

8 ounces crab meat, flaked
2 tablespoons oil
1 cup green peas, cooked and drained
1 cup mushrooms
2 tablespoons green onion, minced
1 tablespoon green pepper, minced
1 teaspoon fresh cilantro, minced
4 eggs, beaten
1 teaspoon sherry

Stir fry in skillet vegetables and crab in oil. Season eggs. Add sherry. Pour over crab mixture. Cook like a pancake. Turn to brown sides. Cut in wedges and serve.

Serves four.

CRAB QUICHE

1 cup crab meat
3 eggs, beaten
3/4 cup cream
1 9 inch pie shell, partially baked
1/4 cup Swiss cheese, grated
pinch of salt
pinch of pepper
2 drops Tabasco
2 tablespoons chives, chopped

Blend eggs and cream. Place crab in bottom of shell and sprinkle with cheese. Mix salt, pepper, Tabasco and chives to eggs. Pour over crab. Bake at 350 degrees for 40 minutes until center is done.
Serves four.

CRAB, SHRIMP AND RICE CASSEROLE

1 1/2 pounds crab meat
1 pound cooked shrimp, shelled and deveined
1/4 green pepper, chopped
1/3 cup parsley, chopped
2 cups rice, cooked
1 1/2 cups mayonnaise
2 packages frozen peas, thawed
3/4 teaspoon salt
1/3 teaspoon white pepper

Toss in a 6 quart butter casserole all ingredients. Bake covered at 350 degrees for 60 minutes.
Serves six.

CRAB SOUFFLE

1 pound crab meat, flaked
1 teaspoon lemon, grated
1 cup mayonnaise
1 small onion, chopped
1 cup celery, chopped
1/4 cup green pepper, chopped
1 can pimiento, chopped
10 slices white bread
4 eggs
3 cups milk
1 teaspoon salt
1/4 teaspoon pepper
1/4 teaspoon dry mustard
1 (10 ounce) can mushroom soup
1 teaspoon paprika
1/2 cup Cheddar cheese, grated

   Mix lemon with mayonnaise, onion, celery, pepper and pimiento. Gently mix crab with vegetables.
   Remove bread crusts and dice bread. Layer bread and crab in a shallow buttered casserole.
   Beat eggs with milk, salt, pepper and mustard. Pour into casserole. Cover and refrigerate four hours.
   Bake at 325 degrees for 60 minutes. Mix soup with paprika and boil. Uncover casserole and pour soup over top. Sprinkle with cheese and bake uncovered 15 for 15 minutes.
   Serves four.

CRAB TOSTADAS

8 ounces crab meat, flaked
1 medium tomato, diced
1/2 avocado, peeled and sliced
3 green onions, sliced
1 tablespoon lemon juice
1/4 teaspoon salt
1/4 teaspoon hot pepper sauce
1 tablespoon oil
4 corn tortillas
1 cup lettuce, shredded
1 cup sharp cheddar cheese, shredded

Combine crab, tomato, avocado, onions, lemon juice, salt and pepper sauce. Chill.

Heat in skillet oil. Turn tortillas in hot oil quickly until soft. Place into custard cup to shape. Bake at 350 degrees eight minutes until crisp.

Divide lettuce among tortilla shells and top with cheese and crab salad.

Serves four.

CRAB WITH VERA CRUZ SAUCE

1 pound crab meat, flaked
1 small onion, chopped
3 cloves garlic, minced
2 tablespoons oil
2 cups tomatoes, peeled and chopped
1/4 cup fresh parsley, chopped
dash of cloves
dash of cinnamon
4 drops Tabasco
1 teaspoon Dijon mustard
3 tablespoons almond, ground
2 teaspoons capers
1 small can pimiento, chopped
1/4 cup green olives, chopped
3 tablespoons butter
2 cups rice, cooked

Sauté onion and garlic in oil. Add tomatoes, parsley, spices, Tabasco, mustard and almonds. Simmer and stir for five minutes. Add capers, pimiento and olives. Reduce heat to warm.

Saute in butter crab until hot. Serve crab on rice with sauce over both.

Serves four.

DEVILED CRAB

1 pound crab meat, flaked
2 tablespoons onion, chopped
2 tablespoons butter
2 tablespoons flour
3/4 cup milk
1 tablespoon lemon juice
1 1/2 teaspoons dry mustard
1 teaspoon Worcestershire sauce
1/2 teaspoon salt
3 drops Tabasco
pepper to taste
cayenne to taste
1 egg, beaten
1 tablespoon parsley, chopped
1/4 cup dry bread crumbs
1 tablespoon butter

Sauté onion in butter. Add flour. Add milk gradually and cook until thick, stir constantly. Add lemon juice and seasonings. Blend in egg. Add crab and parsley. Blend well. Place in six custard cups. Sprinkle with a butter crumb mixture. Bake at 350 degrees for 25 minutes until brown.

Serves six.

GLACIER BAY DEVILED CRAB

1 pound crab meat, flaked
1 onion, chopped fine
1 stalk celery, chopped fine
1/4 cup green pepper, chopped fine
1/4 cup red pepper, chopped fine
1 clove garlic, minced
1/2 cup olive oil
1 tablespoon scallions, chopped fine
1/2 teaspoon Worcestershire sauce
1 tablespoon prepared mustard
dash Tabasco sauce
salt to taste
white pepper to taste
1/4 cup sherry
1/4 cup milk
2 eggs, beaten lightly
2 tablespoons bread crumbs
paprika for garnish
fresh parsley, chopped for garnish

Sauté in oil onion, celery, peppers and garlic. Add crab, scallions, Worcestershire sauce, mustard, Tabasco, salt, pepper, sherry and milk. Bring to a boil. Remove from heat. Add eggs and crumbs. Mix well.

Place in 2 quart casserole. Add garnish. Broil for seven minutes.

Serves four.

HALIBUT STUFFED WITH ALASKAN CRAB

1/4 pound crab meat, flaked
1 pound halibut fillet or steak
2 slices bacon, chopped fine
1 tablespoon butter
2 stalks celery, diced
1/2 cup mushrooms, sliced
1/4 cup dried onion
1 teaspoon fresh thyme, chopped
1 teaspoon fresh parsley, chopped
1 egg
salt to taste
pepper to taste

caper butter
1/4 pound butter, softened
2 tablespoons capers, chopped
1 tablespoon shallots, chopped
2 tablespoons lemon juice
1teaspoon fresh dill, chopped
1 teaspoon Dijon mustard

To make caper butter, mix 1/4 pound with capers, shallots, lemon juice, dill and mustard. Set aside.

Sauté bacon in butter until brown. Add celery, onions and mushrooms.

When tender add crab, salt, pepper and herbs. Remove from heat and mix in egg. Set aside to cool. Cut a pocket in halibut and stuff with crab mixture. Grill until halibut flakes. Top with caper butter.

Serves two.

HAM STUFFED WITH CRAB

3 pounds crab meat
1/2 cup butter
20 slices ham
3 tablespoons lemon juice
1 1/2 teaspoons salt
1/2 teaspoon fresh ground white pepper
1 tablespoon fresh parsley, chopped for garnish

Sauté in skillet ham slices on both sides in butter. Line baking dish with ham. Keep warm.

Add to skillet remaining butter, crab, juice, salt and pepper. Toss over high heat for five minutes. Pile mixture in baking dish and garnish.

Serves six.

HAM STUFFED WITH CRAB

8 ounces crab meat, flaked
6 thin slices boiled ham
1 package white sauce mix
1/4 teaspoon curry powder
1 teaspoon sherry
2 cups rice, cooked
green onion, sliced for garnish

Divide crab over ham slices. Roll up and secure with a wood toothpick. Place on baking pan seam side down. Bake at 350 degrees for 20 minutes.

Prepare white sauce a directed on package. Add curry powder and sherry. Arrange ham rolls on bed of rice. Spoon sauce over rolls. Garnish.

Serves two.

HOT CRAB SOUFFLE

1 pound crab meat, flaked
3 tablespoons butter
1/4 cup flour
1 1/2 teaspoon spicy mustard
1 cup milk
3 egg yolks, beaten
3 egg whites, beaten
2 tablespoons parsley, chopped
2 tablespoons onion, minced
1 tablespoon lemon juice
3 drops Tabasco

Melt butter. Blend in four and seasonings. Add milk. Cook and stir until thick and smooth.

Stir Tabasco into egg yolks. Add to remaining sauce and stir constantly. Add parsley, onion, lemon and crab. Fold in egg whites. Place in buttered 1 1/2 quart casserole. Place casserole in pan of hot water. Bake at 350 degrees for 60 minutes until souffle is firm in the center.

Serves six.

MOUSSE OF CRAB

1 cup crab meat, flaked
1 pound halibut fillet
3/4 cup butter, diced
2 eggs
2 egg yolks
1/2 tablespoon fresh chervil, chopped
1 tablespoon parsley, chopped fine
pinch nutmeg
1/4 cups whipped cream
tablespoons Cognac
salt to taste
pepper to taste

Pound halibut in mortar until smooth. Force through a strainer and mortar again.

Gradually add butter, eggs, yolks, chervil and parsley. Season. Mix or 15 minutes with a wooden spatula in a bowl over ice. Stir in whipped cream, Cognac and crab. Turn mixture into a buttered ring mold. Poach over hot water for 35 minutes.

Serves six.

PACIFIC CRAB CAKES

1 pound crab meat, flaked
2 cups water
2 cups instant mashed potatoes
2 tablespoons butter
1/4 cup onion, minced
1 tablespoon mayonnaise
1 1/4 teaspoon salt
1 1/4 crab seasoning
1 tablespoon Worcestershire sauce
1 tablespoon baking powder
1 egg
1 egg white
oil for frying

Prepare instant potatoes in boiling water and butter. Let cool in refrigerator.

Combine chilled potatoes, crab and onion. Add remaining ingredients. Chill four hours.

Make crab patties. Fry in hot oil until golden.

Serves six.

PANCAKES WITH CRAB FILLING

8 ounces crab meat
1 cup whole kernel corn, drained
2 cups white sauce
pepper to taste
1/4 cup Swiss cheese, grated
2 tablespoons parsley, chopped for garnish
8 pancakes
salt to taste

Mix crab and corn with one cup white sauce. Season. Divide mixture between eight pancakes. Fold in half and place in baking dish. Sprinkle with cheese. Bake at 400 degrees for 20 minutes. Pour over remaining white sauce and garnish.

Serves four.

SCRAMBLED CRAB AND EGGS

1 pound crab meat, flaked
1/4 cup onion, chopped
1/4 cup bacon
4 eggs, beaten
1/4 cup milk
3/4 teaspoon salt
dash of pepper
6 slices toast, buttered

Fry bacon until brown. Add onion and cook until tender. Combine eggs, milk, seasonings and crab. Add to onion mixture and cook until eggs are firm.

Serves six.

SEWARD CRAB BAKE

1 pound crab meat, flaked
1/4 cup butter
2 tablespoons flour
1 cup cream
1 teaspoon prepared mustard
1/2 teaspoon salt
1/4 teaspoon pepper
1/4 teaspoon mace
1 tablespoon lemon juice
1 pound carrots, sliced
2 hard boiled eggs, chopped fine
2 cups bread crumbs
2 tablespoons butter, melted
lemon wedges for garnish

Melt butter in sauce pan. Stir in flour. Cook and stir over low heat until smooth and bubbly. Remove from heat. Stir in cream. Heat and stir until boiling. Fold in seasonings, carrots, crab and eggs. Pour mixture into 1 1/2 quart casserole. Toss butter and crumbs and sprinkle over top of casserole. Bake at 350 degrees for 45 minutes until bubbly. Garnish.

Serves four.

SPAGHETTI WITH CRAB SAUCE

1 pound crab meat, flaked
4 cloves garlic, minced
1/2 cup butter
2 tablespoons olive oil
1 cup green onion, sliced
2 medium tomatoes, diced
1/2 cup parsley, chopped
2 tablespoons lemon juice
1/2 teaspoon Italian dressing
1/2 teaspoon salt
1 pound spaghetti, cooked

Sauté garlic in butter and oil. Add remaining ingredients except spaghetti. Simmer for ten minutes. Toss spaghetti with crab mixture. Serve with grated Parmesan cheese.
Serves six.

SPICY CRAB CAKES

1 pound crab meat, flaked
1 egg, beaten lightly
1 1/2 teaspoons Dijon mustard
2 tablespoons shallots, minced
2 tablespoons parsley, minced
6 tablespoons mayonnaise
2 tablespoons lemon juice
1 1/2 cups bread crumbs
1/4 pound butter
1/4 cup oil for frying
cayenne to taste

Mix crab, egg, mustard, cayenne, scallion, parsley, mayonnaise and lemon juice. Shape 12 patties 1/2 inch thick. Roll in crumbs. Fry in oil until golden. Drain on paper towels. Serve hot.
Serves four.

STUFFED CRAB AU GRATIN

**1 pound crab meat, flaked
1 medium onion, chopped
1/3 cup red pepper, chopped fine
1 tablespoon olive oil
1 tablespoon butter
2 tablespoons water
1/2 cup dry bread crumbs
1/3 cup mayonnaise
3 tablespoons black olives, chopped
3 tablespoons cream
3 tablespoons port
1 tablespoon Dijon mustard
1 tablespoon lemon juice
1 tablespoon parsley, chopped
1/2 teaspoon salt
1/4 teaspoon hot pepper sauce
1/8 teaspoon pepper
3/4 cup bread crumbs for topping
2 tablespoons Parmesan cheese, grated for topping**

Sauté in oil onion, carrot and red pepper. Add water. Cover. Turn heat to lowest point and steam for 15 minutes.

Place all remaining ingredients except those for topping in a large bowl. toss and mix lightly. Add skillet mixture and toss again. Mound mixture into six baking dishes. Combine topping ingredients and top each dish. Bake at 400 degrees for 20 minutes until brown.

Serves six.

ORDER FORM

AK Enterprises Books

Please fill out this form and return to:

AK Enterprises
P.O. Box 210241
Anchorage, Alaska 99521-0241

Please send me_____copies of
Alaska Shrimp and Crab Recipes . . . . **$14.95 each**

Please send me_____copies of
Alaskan Halibut Recipes . . . . **$14.95 each**

Please send me_____copies of
Salmon Recipes from Alaska . . . . **$14.95 each**

Please send me_____copies of
Moose and Caribou Recipes from Alaska . . **$13.95 each**

Total amount for books: $_____

$3.00 per book for postage/handling
    Note: Canadian orders - please add an additional $3.50 $_____
    for Shipping and Handling

Total amount enclosed: $_____

Send books to:

Name: _____

Address: _____

City: _____

State/Zip: _____

Thank you very much for your order. Good cooking!
VISIT US ON THE WEB: alaskacookbook.com

AK Enterprises Books

Please fill out this form and return to:

AK Enterprises
P.O. Box 210241
Anchorage, Alaska 99521-0241

Please send me_____copies of
Alaska Shrimp and Crab Recipes . . . . **$14.95 each**

Please send me_____copies of
Alaskan Halibut Recipes . . . . **$14.95 each**

Please send me_____copies of
Salmon Recipes from Alaska . . . . **$14.95 each**

Please send me_____copies of
Moose and Caribou Recipes from Alaska . . **$13.95 each**

Total amount for books: $_____

$3.00 per book for postage/handling
Note: Canadian orders - please add an additional $3.50 $_____
for Shipping and Handling

Total amount enclosed: $_____

Send books to:

Name: _____

Address: _____

City: _____

State/Zip: _____

Thank you very much for your order. Good cooking!
VISIT US ON THE WEB: alaskacookbook.com